THE GREAT POTATO COOKBOOK

A COLLECTION OF INTERNATIONAL RECIPES FROM THE FOLLOWING COUNTRIES

ARGENTINA · AUSTRALIA · AUSTRIA

BELGIUM · BERMUDA · CANADA · CZECHOSLOVAKIA

DENMARK · ENGLAND · FINLAND · FRANCE · GERMANY

GREECE · HOLLAND · HONG KONG · HUNGARY · INDIA

INDONESIA · IRAN · IRELAND · ITALY · JAMAICA

LUXEMBOURG · MALAYSIA · MEXICO · MOROCCO

NEW ZEALAND · NORWAY · PAKISTAN · POLAND

PORTUGAL · SCOTLAND · SOUTH AFRICA

SPAIN · SUMATRA · SWEDEN

SWITZERLAND · TUNISIA · TURKEY

UNITED STATES OF AMERICA · U.S.S.R. · WALES

YUGOSLAVIA

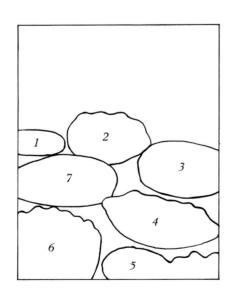

Front Cover

1. *Jean Ross's potato and ham bone soup, see page 45.*
2. *Chocolate profiteroles, see page 116.*
3. *Potato and asparagus quiche, see page 74.*
4. *Spicy potato skins, Straw potatoes and crisps,*
   see pages 18 and 19.
5. *Coquilles St Jacques, see page 83.*
6. *Hot potato and parsley salad, see page 24.*
7. *Mixed meats with olives, raisins and potatoes, see page 94.*

Jennifer Steel

THE GREAT
POTATO
COOKBOOK

Recipes from around the world

Search Press

First published in Great Britain 1989
Search Press Ltd,
Wellwood, North Farm Road, Tunbridge Wells, Kent TN2 3DR

The author and publishers would like to thank the department store R.W. Weekes
Ltd of Mount Pleasant, Tunbridge Wells for providing the glass bowl for
photography shown on page 17,
and Robert Dyas Ltd of 24/32, Gabriel's Hill, Maidstone, Kent, for providing items
for photography shown on pages 81, 123, 137.

Photography by Search Press Studios, with the exception of the photographs taken
by the Potato Marketing Board of 50, Hans Crescent, Knightsbridge, London SW1
0NB. The author and publishers acknowledge with thanks the Potato Marketing
Board for giving their permission for their photographs to be reproduced on pages
31, 35, 49 (above), 54, 56, 68, 70, 72, 76, 95, 99, 101, 104, 107, 121, 132.

ISBN 0 85532 595 X

Photoset by Scribe Design, 123 Watling Street, Gillingham, Kent ME7 2YY
Made and printed in Spain by Artes Graphicas Elkar, S. Coop.

Contents

Introduction
page 7

Hors d'Oeuvres and salads
page 16

Soups
page 36

Classic recipes and side dishes
page 48

Main meals and supper dishes
page 64

Baked potatoes
page 100

Sweet potatoes
page 108

Puddings, pies, cakes and pastries
page 114

Breads, scones and pancakes
page 126

Wine
page 136

Indexes
page 141

With love to my husband Harry

I would like to thank the many kind friends who have helped me in the preparation of this book. Sadly, they are too numerous to list but my especial thanks go to the Martins of Bilbao for their interesting family recipes; to my very good friend, Teresa Davy, for her unfailing assistance in the typing of the manuscript, also her well-founded criticism and encouragement; to Julie Wood who designed the book and assisted greatly at the photography sessions and last, but not least, to my colleagues at Search Press who, having conned me into writing this book in the first place, have been unstinting in their support.

Introduction

It would be difficult to imagine a world without potatoes but wherever you may be today in Europe, North America or Australasia, go back only two centuries and you would find such a world. In just this short span of time, the potato has progressed from being regarded as an exotic botanical oddity to the dining table of millions.

The story of the potato is a strange one, often told as a romantic parallel to that of tobacco; a New World novelty brought back by swashbuckling explorers to intrigue a Virgin Queen. But this is not so and Sir Walter Raleigh was not the first to bring the potato to Europe. Nearly half a century before Raleigh planted his first crop in Ireland, potatoes had been imported into France, and even earlier into Spain. Incredibly, for a country so noted for its gastronomic ingenuity, France did not grow the potato primarily as a food source, but for its flower.

Spain, with its strong ties with South America, was almost certainly the first European country to have adopted the potato as a food and to have recognised its storage potential. This was essential at a time when an Atlantic crossing took many weeks, during which time no green vegetables remained palatable. Though far from rich in vitamin C, which keeps the scourge of scurvy at bay, the potato did help to delay the onset of this debilitating disease. Even Raleigh is believed to have realised this, well over a century before scurvy decimated Anson's circumnavigating crew, during their four year voyage from 1740 to 1744.

The origins of the potato can be traced to the remote sierras of the high Peruvian Andes. It was grown as the staple food by the Incas who lived in the heights and who are known to have successfully cultivated the potato at altitudes as great as 4,572 metres/15,000 feet. In the lower regions, the potato was rarely a part of the diet, as the lowland Indians grew and ate maize, which they preferred. The British, French and Spanish seafarers, who took vast quantities of gold from South America to Europe, also took the potato from Peru.

It is remarkable that a vegetable native to so rarified an atmosphere should adapt so readily to rain-swept maritime Ireland, the sea-level plains of the Low Countries and most of Western and Central Europe. For more than two hundred years the potato remained a culinary oddity, linked with the spread of leprosy and at one time banned in Eastern France, in the region of the Jura Mountains, by the governors of Besançon. Fear of the potato as a health hazard persisted in France almost until the nineteenth century and was only allayed when the level-headed economist and agronomist, Antoine-Auguste Parmentier, resorted to science to show that former fears were unfounded. The continuing craze for potato flowers as gifts indicates that trepidation persisted and that then, as now, people took their science with a pinch of salt! It was left to the pioneering work of Parmentier and the scarcity of other foods to establish the potato as a staple part of the French diet during the Revolution and the Napoleonic wars.

Widespread suspicion of the potato did not affect the British Isles. It is likely that the potato's reputation as an aphrodisiac alarmed the stolid citizens more than its culinary short-comings! It was therefore not until the late 1720s that the first open fields of potatoes were sown, significantly in Scotland. Only with the Industrial Revolution and the movement of people away from the land to the towns did the potato begin to make its full impact on British eating habits.

In an age before refrigeration, the storage properties of the potato were a vital asset, enabling the frugal housewife to lay up a store for the winter months. Potatoes could be grown on the smallest plot of land and seemed to flourish even in poor soil. Being firm and dense, and not over-subject to bruising, they could be conveyed from one area to another by ship, cart or train. Thus, the potato, once served to the gentry and royalty of nations, became the staple food of the working classes. On a diet of bread, onions, turnips, carrots and potatoes, the masses that built industrial Europe went to work, raised their families and, once in a while, if poverty had been kept at bay, enjoyed a joint of meat.

Much of the culture of the potato in Britain dates from Victorian times, with its emphasis on good, hearty appetites. Recipes were handed down from mother to daughter, how to roast, bake and boil and the potato was served with every meal. The age of meat, two veg, and potatoes boiled or mashed is still remembered with affection by an older generation. Fads in food come and go, just as with fashion, but tried-and-true dishes such as sausage and mash, fish and chips, crisps and jacket potatoes will still be around in the next century. The popularity of the jacket potato, in fact, owes much to a technological breakthrough during the second world war and the invention of the magnetron. Its purpose was to solve the riddle of the microwave, a potent source of radio energy that possessed the lethal property of heating from within. The rest is history and the potato emerged as the ideal natural convenience food, hygienically packed in its own skin and retaining all its taste and goodness, when cooked in a microwave oven.

Today the potato is prized as much for its versatility as its nutrients. Robust, enduring, adaptable and filling, it can be cooked in an endless variety of ways and served with more main courses than would have seemed possible to our parents. Its detractors would have us believe that it is fattening, in spite of the fact that it only contains about 20 per cent of dry matter. In the average diet, potatoes provide less than 10 per cent of our total carbohydrate intake and, in fact, contain less sugar than bread, most biscuits and pasta.

In writing this book, I have endeavoured to provide a wide variety of dishes either prepared wholly from potatoes, or potatoes mixed with other ingredients. I have included tasty meals from my childhood, exotic dishes I have enjoyed in many different countries and recipes acquired from friends and acquaintances. The contents are therefore a mixture of traditional favourites and international dishes which may not be so familiar. Whatever the country of origin, I have used ingredients that are now readily available and have stressed the importance of purchasing fresh vegetables and herbs, whenever possible.

Since I began to collect these recipes, the old saying 'there is nothing new under the sun', has taken on a whole new meaning for me. On learning of the project, friends, colleagues and almost complete strangers kindly gave me details of what they considered to be their own specialities but, so often, I have found identical recipes under a different name.

It has been extremely difficult to determine exactly which recipes to include and although no cookery book of this type can claim to be complete, I hope I have reached a happy compromise by taking a fresh look at the ways in which potatoes can be used. The recipes come from many lands and you will doubtless be able to add your own special favourites to the list. I well remember a rainy night in Rotterdam, when a neat paper cone of 'frites' topped with creamy mayonnaise added a new meaning to the phrase 'chips with everything'. The resilient potato has survived years of neglect and being regarded as a rather boring staple food. Now it is time to realise its full potential!

Pick a potato

Potatoes serve a useful 'give-and-take' purpose in recipes, as they add flavour, quantity and moisture without detracting from the accompanying ingredients. This is especially helpful in rechauffé dishes, such as fish cakes or Durham cutlets.

Although considered mainly as a savoury ingredient, the advantages of adding potatoes to bread, cakes and puddings should not be overlooked. Their moisture and starch content are essential to the recipes given in this book.

Types of potatoes

In general, varieties of potatoes are divided into two main groups; waxy and floury. The waxy potato is ideal for frying and serving cold in salads but for boiling, mashing and baking, the floury potato is the better choice.

Sweet potatoes are considered a delicacy in many parts of the world and the Maoris of New Zealand cook them as a vegetable. On a nest of stones a wood fire is lit and when the fire has died down, the sweet potatoes, wrapped in palm leaves, are placed on the stones. They are then covered with wet sacking and left to steam for at least two hours. You can cook them in the same way as an ordinary baked potato! They are declicious with all white meat dishes.

How to buy potatoes

All varieties are available in quantities ranging from 450g (1 lb) to 50.8kg (1 cwt). When buying maincrop potatoes in bulk, make sure they are from a reputable trader, or the money you save with this method of purchase will be offset by the number of rotten potatoes you have to throw away.

Only buy sufficient early potatoes for your immediate use. They should not be stored or they will lose their delicious flavour.

How to handle potatoes

Handle potatoes with care. If they have been supplied in a plastic bag, remove this as soon as possible and store in a brown paper bag, or covered basket container.

Keep in a cool, dry place out of direct light. Undue warmth will cause sprouting and softening; moisture will cause rot; light will cause greening and frost will cause general damage. Do not keep near any strong-smelling goods or the potatoes will become tainted.

How to prepare potatoes in advance

Feast days and festivals are occasions when potatoes may have to be prepared in advance and stored, so that you can spend more time with your guests. The day beforehand, peel sufficient quantities to last for the holiday period, place them in a deep bucket, sprinkle with coarse rock salt and cover with cold water. Put the bucket in a dark, cool area and change the water and salt solution each day. The potatoes will remain fresh for up to three days without going slimy. Do rinse the required amount of potatoes in fresh cold water before cooking.

How to cook potatoes

The humble potato has been the staff of life for many generations but, as with all fresh vegetables, it is the manner in which it is cooked that brings out its flavour.

OLD POTATOES

There are six basic ways of cooking old potatoes to retain their flavour.

Peeled and boiled: always use potatoes of equal size and peel as thinly as possible. Place in a bowl of lightly salted cold water for about 30 minutes before cooking. To cook the potatoes, put into fresh cold water and add about one teaspoonful of salt to each 570ml (pint) of water and bring to the boil. When cooked, strain off the water, noting that it can be saved for use in soups or gravy. Lay a clean, folded tea towel over the potatoes. This will absorb the steam, leaving the potatoes dry or floury, depending on the type used.

Peeled and steamed: proceed as for peeled and boiled potatoes but to cook them, place into a steamer over boiling water. Cover with a lid and steam until cooked, taking care to keep the water at boiling point and topping up with boiling water when necessary.

Boiled without peeling: wash the potatoes thoroughly and cut off a small piece at one end to prevent bursting. Steep the potatoes in cold salted water for 30 minutes, drain and put into fresh cold salted water. Bring to the boil and cook for 20 to 30 minutes, until tender. Drain off the water. Lay a clean, folded tea towel over the potatoes to absorb the steam. Potatoes cooked in this way may be served in their jackets or peeled.

Baked in their jackets in the oven: the larger the potatoes the better but they should be of even size. Wash thoroughly, dry and then bake in a hot oven for 1½ to 2 hours. If you prefer, they can be rolled in coarse salt after they have been dried. Do not over-bake the potatoes or they will shrivel up.

Fried in deep fat or oil: potatoes cooked by this method are better known as 'chips' or 'French fries'. They are first cooked in moderately hot fat, drained and then replaced in the fat which has been brought to a higher temperature.

Do not try to deep-fry too many chips at once. To test the temperature of the fat, drop a small cube of bread into it. This should sizzle immediately in a moderate heat but will brown very quickly if the fat is too hot. Waxy potatoes make the best chips and they should be cut into strips of even thickness.

Opinions differ as to the advisability of soaking the potatoes in cold salted water before cooking. If you decide to do this, be very careful to dry them thoroughly before immersing in the hot fat.

Roasted: even-sized potatoes should be peeled and par-boiled for about 8 minutes. Drain and dry off. Score the surface of the potatoes with a fork and place into hot fat, either round a joint of meat, or in a separate pan of hot fat, basting well before **roasting**.

NEW POTATOES

New potatoes should be scraped, not peeled. Best of all, wash them and cook them in their skins. If the skins are tough, they may be removed after cooking.

To cook new potatoes, place in boiling salted water with a sprig or two of fresh mint and boil for 10 to 15 minutes, or until tender. Drain thoroughly, add a good sized knob of butter and some finely chopped mint.

New potatoes on Christmas Day! If this idea appeals to you, cover the base of a deep biscuit tin with dry sawdust, place a layer of new potatoes on the sawdust being careful not to let them touch each other. Cover with another layer of sawdust about 2.5cm (1in) deep, then more potatoes until the tin is full, finishing with a layer of sawdust. Put the lid on the tin and seal all around with adhesive tape. Bury the tin in a cool spot in the garden – remember to mark the position! – and lift a few days before Christmas.

Sweet potatoes

Always choose chunky, medium-sized sweet potatoes, which are smooth of skin, firm to the touch and with tapered ends. Avoid any potatoes with decayed spots, as even when you cut away the bad bits, the flavour of the remaining flesh will have been affected.

Sweet potatoes do not keep as well as ordinary ones, so it is advisable to purchase only what you require at the time. If you do need to store some, however, keep them in a dry, cool, well-ventilated place.

Sweet potatoes are of two types. The dry, floury sweet potato has a light brown skin and pale flesh which is similar to an ordinary white potato in texture. The more moist variety, sometimes referred to as 'yams', have reddish-brown skins, orange-coloured flesh and are more readily available.

Useful facts and abbreviations

All quantities in this book are given in metric and imperial measures. When making any recipe, only use one set of measures as they are not interchangeable. Exact conversions from imperial to metric measures are not possible, so the metric measures have been rounded up in units of 5, 10, 15, 20 or 25.

Oven Temperatures

Gas Mark		°F	°C
½	very cool	250	120
1	cool	275	140
2	cool	300	150
3	moderate	325	160
4	moderate	350	180
5	moderately hot	375	190
6	moderately hot	400	200
7	hot	425	220
8	hot	450	230
9	very hot	475	240

Measurements

Inches	Centimetres
¼	0.5
½	1
¾	2
1	2.5
1¼	3
1½	4
1¾	4.5
2	5
3	7.5
4	10
5	13
6	15
7	18

Volume

Fluid ounces	Pints	Millilitres
2	–	55
3	–	75
4	–	110
5	¼	150
6	–	175
7	–	200
8	–	225
10	½	275
12	–	330
15	¾	425
18	–	500
20	1	600
–	1½	900
–	1¾	1 litre

Weights

Ounces	Pounds	Grammes
½	–	10
1	–	25
1½	–	40
2	–	50
2½	–	60
3	–	75
4	–	110
4½	–	125
5	–	150
6	–	175
7	–	200
8	–	225
9	–	250
10	–	275
12	–	350
–	1	450
–	1½	700
–	2	900
–	3	1 kg 350g

When converting quantities over 450g (1lb) to Imperial weights, add the total number of grammes, then adjust to the nearest unit of 25. As a guide, 1000g (1kg) equals about 2lbs 3oz.

Notes for American and Australian users

Fluid measures

The 8 fl oz measuring cup is used in America. In Australia metric measures are now used in conjunction with the standard 250ml measuring cup. The Imperial pint, used in Britain and Australia, is 20 fl oz, while the American pint is 16 fl oz.

Spoon measures

One important point to remember is that the Australian tablespoon differs from both the British and American tablespoons; the table below gives a comparison. The British standard tablespoon has been used throughout this book and holds 17.7 ml, the American 14.2 ml, and the Australian 20 ml. A teaspoon holds about 5 ml in all three countries.

An Imperial and American guide to solid and liquid measures

Imperial	American
Solid measures	
1lb butter or margarine	2 cups
1lb flour	4 cups
1lb granulated or caster sugar	2 cups
1lb icing sugar	3 cups
8oz rice	1 cup

Imperial	American
Liquid measures	
¼ cup liquid	⅔ cup liquid
½ pint	1¼ cups
¾ pint	2 cups
1 pint	2½ cups
1½ pints	3¾ cups
2 pints	5 cups

Abbreviations

cm	centimetre(s)
in	inch(es)
ml	millilitre(s)
tsp	teaspoon(sful)
dsp	dessertspoon(sful)
tbsp	tablespoon(sful)
lt	litre(s)
fl oz	fluid ounce(s)
pt	pint(s)
lb	pound(s)
kg	kilogram(s)
g	gramme(s)
cwt	hundredweight(s)
mm	millimetre(s)

Potato potpourri

The humble 'spud' is not just a superb culinary ingredient which can be used in a wide variety of recipes, from salads, soups and main dishes to cakes, bread and puddings, but also has many other uses.

Removing mud stains: allow mud to dry then brush out as much as possible. Using water in which potatoes have been boiled, carefully sponge out the remaining dirt.

Dying leather: before applying any dye to leather, rub the item to be dyed all over with the cut side of a potato. Allow to dry thoroughly, then apply the dye.

Cleaning oil paintings: use the cut side of a potato dampened with a little cold water and rub this gently over the surface of the painting. Wipe clean with a dampened sponge. Allow to dry and then polish carefully with a piece of silk. The painting should then be gently rubbed all over with a flannel cloth, on to which a little linseed oil has been sprinkled.

Lessening oversalting: if a stew or soup is too salty, add one or two potatoes to absorb the salt while the stew is still cooking.

Carpet burn: on a wool carpet, rub the burn immediately with a slice of raw potato, which removes the surface singeing. The brown tips left on the ends of the threads may wash out but, if not, trim them very lightly with nail scissors.

Rheumatism: folklore has it that carrying a whole potato in your pocket will prevent rheumatism – it can't hurt to try it!

Beauty hint: sliced or grated raw potato placed in a muslin bag and applied to the eyes will take away any bags under the eyes.

Cleaning silver: you can clean silver by plunging it into water in which potatoes have been boiled.

De-icing: try half a raw potato to de-ice a frozen windscreen.

Fire lighting: dried potato peelings will help to light a fire.

Keeping tobacco moist: a small piece of potato carried in your tobacco pouch will prevent the tobacco from becoming too dry.

Cleaning a decanter: chopped raw potato and warm water shaken together in a decanter will remove wine stains.

Complexion care: wash a newly dug potato, chill well and cut into thick slices. Rub the slices on your face, particularly the areas around the nose. This treatment cleanses the skin, discourages excess oiliness and is a boon to skins prone to blemishes.

Potato printing: you can make your own labels or letter headings and keep the children amused for hours. Wash and dry a potato and cut in half. Make a printing block by cutting the flat surface of the potato away, so that a square, circle, triangle, or any shape you want is left. Mix some powder or poster paint and cover the surface of the block with paint. Press it gently but firmly on to a sheet of paper until you have the effect you require.

recipes

Hors d'oeuvres and salads

As the name 'Hors d'Oeuvre' suggests, this dish originated in France and was intended to whet the appetite for the meal to follow. As it starts the meal, it should be light enough in content not to spoil the main course, and appealing both in colour and presentation. If you want to enjoy a good, hearty starter, then balance the meal with a fairly light main course.

Salads can mean anything from a main course to a dainty 'nouvelle cuisine' starter. The choice of salad vegetables available today is enormous but these should be freshly purchased and not stored. Again, colour and presentation are very important.

In preparing potato salads, using fresh potatoes, do choose small and waxy potatoes. Some countries, in fact, sell these labelled as 'salad potatoes'. I have found these in various Northern European cities and although perhaps a little more expensive, they are well worth buying. I frequently cause great amusement in my local greengrocer's shop by hand picking small new potatoes just to be used for a salad. In the north of England, notably Yorkshire, these are also known as 'chats'.

Leftover cooked vegetables can also be used in salads. The most classical dish is 'Russian' salad. In this recipe there should always be at least three vegetables and one of these must be peas. I don't usually have any leftover peas, so just defrost some frozen ones whenever I want to make this recipe. No specific quantities are necessary – just mix the cold vegetables together with some good quality mayonnaise, add a little cream and season to taste with salt and pepper. Chill well before serving!

Bon appétit!

Opposite: see page 32 for Creole potato salad recipe.

Spicy potato skins
Australia

(see above)

225g (8oz) potato skins
50g (2oz) plain flour
1 medium egg, beaten
150ml (5fl oz) milk and water
  mixed
Pinch of salt
½ tsp curry powder
Oil or fat to deep fry

Dry the potato skins thoroughly with kitchen paper. Make a thin, coating batter with the flour, egg, milk and water, salt and the curry powder. Take care not to add all the liquid at one time as you may find you do not require quite the full amount. It depends on the flour.

Heat the oil or fat until a blue haze can be seen, then dip the potato skins in the batter and deep fry in the oil. Do not put too many into the oil at one time. When crisp and golden, remove from the oil and drain on kitchen paper.

Waxy or floury potatoes. Serves 4.

This is a tasty way of using up an item that is usually discarded or, at best, thrown on the compost heap. Serving cooked potato skins with drinks, or simply as a starter with, say, a savoury dip can cause quite a few comments!

Straw potatoes

England

(see opposite)

450g (1 lb) potatoes, peeled
Fat or oil for deep frying
Salt

Cut the potatoes into thin, even sized straws 6mm (¼in) wide by 5cm (2in) long. Wash in cold water and dry thoroughly with a clean tea towel.

Place a small quantity at a time in a chip basket and deep fry until crisp and golden in colour.

Remove from fat or oil and drain. Sprinkle with salt and serve.

Waxy or floury potatoes. Serves 4. Vegetarian dish.

Potato crisps

England

(see opposite)

450g (1 lb) potatoes, peeled
Fat or oil for deep frying
Salt

Slice the peeled potatoes very thinly using a mandolin if available. Wash and dry off on a clean tea towel.

Place a small quantity in a chip basket and deep fry until crisp and golden taking care to turn them over from time to time.

Remove from the fat or oil, drain, sprinkle with salt and serve.

Waxy or floury potatoes. Serves 4. Vegetarian dish.

This recipe is not really from England but that is where I am living at present. It is essential to dry off the raw potato slices before immersing them in the hot fat. These crisps will keep for several days if stored in a suitable airtight tin.

Potato fritters (Bolitas de patata)

Spain

450g (1 lb) potatoes, boiled and still hot
2 medium eggs, beaten
175g (6oz) cheese, grated
2 tbsp flour
Salt and freshly ground black pepper to taste
Sufficient oil to deep fry
Parsley, chopped for garnish

Mash potatoes, or pass through a ricer or sieve. Beat in the eggs and cheese, then the flour and seasonings.

Shape into small balls with your hands well floured. Deep fry in oil until crisp and golden. Drain well on kitchen paper and serve hot, garnished with chopped parsley.

Floury potatoes. Serves 6.

These fritters are also useful to serve as canapés.

Potato and egg mayonnaise

Spain

(Patata con huevo duro y mahonesa)

4 large potatoes boiled and sliced
4 medium eggs, hard-boiled and shelled
1 medium onion, finely sliced
150ml (5fl oz) mayonnaise
Sprigs of parsley to garnish

Arrange the potato slices in a suitable serving dish. Quarter the eggs and place on top of the potatoes. Scatter the onion slices over, dress with mayonnaise and garnish with parsley.

Waxy or new potatoes. Serves 4.

Potato slices with caviar

Denmark

(see above)

75ml (3fl oz) vegetable oil
4 medium potatoes
75ml (3fl oz) sour cream
50g (2oz) jar black caviar or red lumpfish
Lemon wedges to garnish

Heat the oven to Gas Mark 9, 475°F (240°C). Divide the oil between two roasting tins. Scrub potatoes thoroughly but do not peel. Cut the potatoes as evenly as possible, into about 2cm (¾in) slices. Rinse under cold water and dry thoroughly.

Coat both sides of the potato slices in the oil in the tins and arrange in a single layer over each tin. Bake in the oven for about 15 minutes or until the potatoes have crisped around the edges and have turned a light brown. Drain on kitchen paper.

Arrange the slices on a suitable serving dish, top each with a blob of soured cream and a ¼ tsp of caviar. Garnish with lemon wedges and serve immediately.

Waxy or new potatoes. Makes about 32 portions.

This is a simple yet very impressive dish.

Potato chutney (Aalu chatni) *India*

700g (1½ lb) potatoes
50g (2oz) raw cane sugar
600ml (1 pt) water
1 tsp ginger root
50g (2oz) onion, chopped
25g (1oz) sultanas
25g (1oz) almonds, chopped
4 tbsp cider vinegar
Sea salt to taste
½ tsp hot chilli powder

Peel and quarter the potatoes. Boil with the sugar in the water. Grate the ginger, mix with the chopped onion, sultanas and almonds. Add to the potatoes and cook for 10 minutes. Stir in the cider vinegar, sea salt and chilli powder.

Lower the heat and allow to simmer gently for a further 15 minutes. Leave to cool. If covered up, this recipe can be kept in a refrigerator for up to 2 weeks.

Waxy or new potatoes. Serves 4. Vegetarian dish.

This chutney recipe is delicious served with any cold meats.

Potato dressing for potato salad *England*

1 large potato, baked
1 tbsp made English mustard
1 tbsp sugar
1 tbsp olive oil
3 tbsp wine vinegar
1 tbsp fresh parsley, chopped
1 tbsp fresh chives, chopped
Salt and good grinding of
   black pepper to taste
Cream or milk

Peel and sieve the baked potato while still warm. Stir in the mustard and sugar. Beat in the oil and vinegar. Add the parsley, chives and seasoning and as much cream or milk needed to mix to a smooth, creamy consistency.

Pour over freshly cooked, diced potatoes and stir carefully to coat. Serve as warm as possible.

Floury potatoes. Serves 4. Vegetarian dish.

Potato salad with wine dressing *Belgium*

1 medium egg yolk, raw
1 medium egg yolk, hard-
   boiled
1 clove garlic, crushed
1 tsp English mustard
1 tsp French mustard
Salt and black pepper
1 tbsp onion, finely chopped
3 tbsp olive oil
2 tbsp wine vinegar
2 tbsp white wine
1 tbsp gherkin, chopped
2 tbsp cream
1 tsp sugar

450g (1 lb) potatoes, cooked

Dressing: mix all the ingredients together. Extra oil, cream and sugar may be added, according to taste.

Salad: slice the cooked potatoes and place in a suitable dish while still hot. Pour the dressing over the potatoes at least 3 hours before serving.

Waxy or new potatoes. Serves 6.

This delicious dressing can be served with any salad.

Potato salad (Kartoffelsalat) *Austria*

450g (1 lb) potatoes, washed
  and boiled in their skins
2 tbsp olive oil
1 dsp onion, chopped
1 tsp parsley, chopped
2 tbsp wine vinegar
Salt and freshly ground black
  pepper to taste
2 tbsp salt herrings, chopped
2 tbsp gherkins, chopped

Peel the potatoes, if preferred, while still hot. Slice into rounds and place in a suitable serving dish. Mix together the olive oil, chopped onion, parsley, wine vinegar, salt and pepper and shake well. Pour this mixture over the potatoes.

Sprinkle the salt herring and gherkins over the dish and chill well before serving.

Waxy or new potatoes. Serves 4.

In Austria this particular recipe is used as an hors d'oeuvre. The Viennese adore these starter dishes and serve them at any time of the day or night. This recipe could be extended to form a main course.

Potato purée salad *France*
(Salade de purée de pommes de terre)

4 medium carrots
4 tbsp vinaigrette
2 tsp French mustard
275g (10oz) cold potatoes,
  mashed
Salt, black pepper, paprika
1 medium egg, hard-boiled
  and sieved

To make vinaigrette, mix 1 tbsp wine vinegar, 3 tbsp olive oil, salt, and freshly ground black pepper to taste.

Peel and grate the carrots and marinate for 1 hour in 2 tbsp of the vinaigrette. Beat the French mustard together with the rest of the vinaigrette and fold in the cold, mashed potato. Season to taste, adding more mustard, salt or pepper if required. The finished purée should be of a thick, creamy consistency.

Serve in a shallow dish piled high in the centre and marked with the prongs of a fork. Garnish with the sieved egg and grated carrot.

Floury potatoes. Serves 4.

Use this tasty recipe to help eke out a quiche, or to accompany any cold meats.

Oriental potato salad *Hong Kong*

Juice from pineapple used in
  salad
150ml (5fl oz) salad oil
1 tbsp dark soy sauce
1 tbsp wine vinegar
Small piece fresh ginger,
  grated
Pinch of salt
Grinding of black pepper

Dressing: put all the ingredients into a jar with a screw top and shake well. Allow to stand for at least 12 hours before using.

450g (1 lb) small new potatoes
225g (8oz) beansprouts
1 medium tin pineapple
  chunks
2 medium carrots, grated
4 spring onions, chopped
1 lettuce

Salad: scrape the potatoes and boil in salted water until just tender. Drain thoroughly and while still hot, pour over the dressing carefully mixing so that the potatoes are coated. Set aside until cold. Mix together the beansprouts, pineapple chunks (cut in half), carrot and spring onions and combine with the potatoes. Line a suitable serving dish with lettuce leaves and place the potato mixture in the centre of the dish. Chill for at least 2 hours.

New potatoes. Serves 4. Vegetarian dish.

Winter potato salad   *Belgium*

450g (1 lb) potatoes, cooked
and diced
1 apple, red-skinned, cored
and diced
110g (4oz) celery, chopped
110g (4oz) onion, finely
chopped
110g (4oz) walnuts, chopped
1 tsp mustard powder
275ml (5fl oz) mayonnaise
Salt and pepper to taste

Mix together the potatoes, apple, celery, onion and walnuts. Add the mustard powder to the mayonnaise with the salt and pepper and mix well.

Pour over the potato mixture and combine all ingredients. Chill well before serving.

Waxy or new potatoes. Serves 6.

My friend, Elise, who lives in the beautiful old town of Bruges, gave me this recipe. Do use the red-skinned type of eating apple, as this gives a lovely colour to the salad.

Hot potato salad   *Holland*

6 rashers streaky bacon
2 tbsp onion, finely chopped
3 tbsp celery, finely chopped
1 tbsp gherkin, finely
chopped
2 tbsp warm water
4 tbsp warm wine vinegar
1 tsp sugar
1 tsp mustard powder
Salt and freshly ground black
pepper
Good pinch paprika
450g (1 lb) potatoes, cooked,
hot and diced

Grill the bacon until crisp and break into small pieces. Put bacon and fat into a frying pan, add onion, celery and gherkin and continue cooking until the onion is transparent but not brown.

Mix together the warm water and wine vinegar. Stir in the sugar, mustard powder, salt, pepper and paprika and add to the bacon mixture. Combine with the freshly cooked potatoes and serve immediately.

Waxy or new potatoes. Serves 4.

Piquant potato salad with fennel   *Australia*

200ml (7fl oz) vegetable juice,
V8 type
2 tbsp apple cider vinegar
2 medium garlic cloves,
crushed
1 dsp lemon juice
Good grinding black pepper
Good pinch salt

450g (1 lb) potatoes, cooked in
skins, peeled and cubed
1 medium bulb fennel, finely
chopped
4 spring onions, finely
chopped
3 tsp fresh basil, or 1 tsp dried
2 tbsp parsley, finely chopped
*Save the green fennel tops for a
garnish.*

Dressing: put all the ingredients into a jar with a screw-top lid. Shake well and leave for at least 12 hours to allow the flavour to develop. Strain the dressing over the potato mixture and stir carefully. Garnish with the fennel tops and parsley.

Waxy or new potatoes. Serves 4. Vegetarian dish.

Salad: leave the potatoes until cold. Mix all the ingredients together, except the fennel tops and the parsley. Chill well before serving.

Hot potato and parsley salad

Austria

(see above)

50g (2oz) butter
Medium bunch spring onions, chopped
450g (1 lb) potatoes, cooked in their skins
Salt and freshly ground black pepper
2 tbsp parsley, finely chopped for garnish

Melt the butter in a deep frying pan, add the chopped spring onions and gently heat through, taking care not to let them brown.

Add the potatoes and seasoning and carefully shake the pan to coat the potatoes with the butter and spring onions. Serve garnished with the chopped parsley.

Waxy or new potatoes. Serves 6. Vegetarian dish.

Beetroot and potato salad *Poland*

4 medium beetroots
2 medium potatoes
2 large spring onions,
    chopped
1 tbsp parsley, chopped
Salt and pepper to taste
Oil and vinegar to dress

Bake the beetroots and the potatoes in the oven until tender. Allow to cool slightly, then skin and slice them. Arrange alternate beetroot and potato slices on a flat serving dish and garnish with the spring onions.

Put the parsley, seasoning, oil and vinegar into a jar with a screwtop lid. Shake well and pour the dressing over the salad.

Waxy or new potatoes. Serves 4. Vegetarian dish.

This is a delicious salad to serve with left-over beef or lamb. I put the whole potatoes and beetroots in the oven to cook when I am roasting meat so that they are ready to make the salad to serve with any cold left-over meat.

Potato and herb salad *Mexico*

4 medium potatoes, peeled,
    cooked, cubed and kept
    warm
1 tbsp olive oil
2 tbsp wine vinegar
½ tsp salt
Good grinding black pepper
½ tsp oregano
½ tsp marjoram
½ tsp thyme
6 large spring onions, finely
    diced for garnish
*If using cold left-over potatoes
slightly warm the dressing before
combining all the ingredients.*

Place the cooked and cubed potatoes into a large salad bowl. Mix together the olive oil, wine vinegar, seasoning and herbs and pour over the warm potatoes. Stir carefully to coat the potatoes and leave to cool.

When cold, garnish with the spring onions.

Waxy or new potatoes. Serves 4. Vegetarian dish.

Dilled potato salad *Norway*

2 tbsp white wine vinegar
1 tsp salt
¼ tsp white pepper
½ tsp dill weed, or to taste
6 tbsp vegetable oil

6 medium potatoes, cooked,
    sliced, kept warm
2 tbsp spring onions, chopped
2 tbsp fresh parsley, chopped
2 tbsp pickled beetroot, diced
2 tbsp chives, chopped

Dressing: prepare the dill dressing by thoroughly mixing all the ingredients together. Set aside to allow the flavours to merge for at least two hours before using.

Salad: mix the potatoes, spring onions, parsley, beetroot and chives together. Pour the dill dressing over the salad, mixing carefully to ensure that the potatoes are covered.

Waxy or new potatoes. Serves 4. Vegetarian dish.

Potato and chilli salad (Alli chat) *India*

1 tbsp cardamon seeds
Cinnamon stick, about 2.5cm (1in)
1 tsp whole cumin seeds
1 tsp cloves
1 tsp black peppercorns
½ tsp grated nutmeg
450g (1 lb) new potatoes, small
2 small green chillies, chopped
2 tbsp lemon juice
½ tsp garam masala
½ tsp caraway seeds, ground
1½ tsp salt

Garam masala: grind all the spices in a coffee grinder, or liquidiser until a fine powder is obtained.

When made, this spice should be stored in a tightly-lidded glass container, away from light and heat. Only make small quantities which will be used up fairly quickly, as the spice becomes less aromatic with age.

Salad: scrub the potatoes and cook them in their skins in boiling, salted water until just tender. When cool enough to handle, peel and slice. Mix together the chopped chillies, which have been deseeded, lemon juice, garam masala, ground caraway seeds and salt. Carefully combine the potatoes and spices. Place in a shallow dish and chill before serving.

New potatoes. Serves 4. Vegetarian dish.

The addition of a sprinkling of caraway seeds gives a delicious texture to this salad.

Potato and vegetable salad with bumbu dressing *Indonesia*

110g (4oz) green cabbage, shredded
110g (4oz) Chinese cabbage, shredded
50g (2oz) bean sprouts
175g (6oz) cauliflower florets
50g (2oz) green beans, sliced
110g (4oz) carrots, cut into matchsticks
110g (4oz) radishes, red and white sliced
110g (4oz) cucumber, cut into matchsticks
110g (4oz) spring onions, sliced
50g (2oz) watercress, chopped
225g (8oz) potatoes, small new, cooked in their skins until just tender
½ small fresh coconut, grated
1 tbsp tomato ketchup
½ tsp chilli powder
1 clove garlic
½ tsp sea salt
Juice of half fresh lime
Some fresh mint, parsley and coriander to garnish

Blanch the cabbage, bean sprouts, cauliflower, green beans and carrots for two minutes then freshen under cold running water until quite cold. Drain thoroughly.

Mix the radishes, cucumber, spring onions, watercress and potatoes in a large bowl, cover and chill while preparing the dressing.

Bumbu dressing: mix together the coconut and ketchup. Pound in a mortar the chilli powder, garlic and sea salt then add to the coconut mixture. Stir in the lime juice and mix well.

Pour the bumbu dressing over the vegetables and mix well. Garnish with the fresh herbs suitably chopped.

New potatoes. Serves 8. Vegetarian dish.

Curried potato and apple salad   *Holland*

225g (8oz) potatoes, boiled
  and cooled
2 crisp eating apples
25g (1oz) sultanas
275ml (10fl oz) mayonnaise
2 tsp curry powder
2 tsp lemon juice
1 tbsp cream
Salt and pepper to taste

Cut the potatoes into small cubes. Peel and core the apples and dice them. Mix together the potatoes, apples and sultanas.

Mix together the mayonnaise, curry powder, lemon juice, cream and seasoning, then combine with the potato mixture. Chill thoroughly before serving.

Waxy or new potatoes. Serves 4.

This salad is particularly delicious with cold poultry or ham.

Potato stuffed apples   *Spain*
(see below)

2 medium potatoes, washed
  and boiled in their skins
4 large cooking apples, cored
  and halved
2 medium egg yolks, beaten
1 tbsp chervil, chopped
1 tbsp parsley, chopped
2 sticks celery, chopped
2 tbsp lemon juice
1 tsp wine vinegar
Salt and pepper to taste

This recipe can also be used as a salad accompaniment to cold meats.

Peel the cooked potatoes and dice them finely. Remove the flesh from the apple halves without breaking the skins. Dice the apple flesh and mix with the potato.

Stir in the beaten egg yolks, herbs, celery, lemon juice, wine vinegar and seasoning. Fill the apple skins with the mixture and serve chilled.

Waxy or new potatoes. Serves 4.

I enjoy the surprised look on the face of my guests when I serve this unusual starter. The recipe was given to me by an amply proportioned lady, who had lots of Spanish potato recipes. By the time I had translated this one I had had enough, which is a pity as it is such a good recipe and I'll never know what others I missed!

Potato salad with peanut dressing   *Indonesia*

1 crisp lettuce

225g (8oz) potatoes, cooked and diced

225g (8oz) green beans, sliced and cooked

2 medium carrots, cut into strips and cooked

175g (6oz) cabbage, finely shredded

2 large tomatoes, skinned

4 medium eggs, hard-boiled

110g (4oz) onion rings, crisply fried

1 small onion, diced

2 tbsp olive oil

2 tsp chilli powder

275ml (10fl oz) water

110g (4oz) peanuts, ground

Salt to taste

1 tbsp wine vinegar

1 tsp sugar

Salad: on a large platter, arrange the lettuce round the outer edge. Then arrange the potatoes, green beans, carrots, cabbage, tomato slices and quartered eggs. Scatter the onion rings over the salad.

Dressing: fry the diced onion in the oil until transparent. Add the chilli powder, water and ground peanuts. Bring to the boil and simmer gently for about 3 minutes, stirring constantly. Add the salt, vinegar and sugar. Allow to cool until just warm, then pour over the vegetables and serve.

Waxy or new potatoes. Serves 6.

Although Indonesian in origin, I first had this lovely salad in Amsterdam. The peanut dressing can be used in other salads or as a dip.

Mixed salad with peanut and chilli dressing   *Malaysia*

225g (8oz) green cabbage

110g (4oz) French beans

225g (8oz) potatoes

225g (8oz) tinned lotus root

275g (10oz) bean curd (tofu)

4 medium eggs, hard-boiled

Salad: shred the cabbage. Slice the beans into 2.5cm (1in) lengths. Bring two pans of water to the boil. Put the cabbage in one and cook for 1 minute, drain and run cold water through it. Put the beans into the second pan and cook for 2 minutes, drain and rinse thoroughly with cold water. Cook the potatoes in their skins in salted water until just tender. Drain, skin and dice. Thinly slice the lotus root, dice the bean curd and cut the eggs into halves.

Carefully arrange the vegetables, eggs, and bean curd on a very large platter and spoon over a little of the dressing. Serve the remainder of the dressing separately.

Waxy or new potatoes. Serves 6.

225g (8oz) peanuts, shelled

50g (2oz) tamarind

2 tsp chilli powder

½ tsp sea salt

1 tbsp tomato ketchup

Dressing: heat the oven to Gas Mark 4, 350°F (180°C). Spread the peanuts on a baking sheet. Bake in the oven for 10 minutes, remove from oven and allow to cool. Grind roughly in a liquidiser or food processor. Put into a bowl. Put the tamarind in a bowl and pour on 150ml (5fl oz) of boiling water. Let it soak for 10 minutes, then rub through a sieve. Mix the tamarind water, chilli powder, salt and ketchup with the peanuts, adding more water if necessary to a make a fairly thick pouring sauce.

Potato and orange salad

Portugal

350g (12oz) new potatoes, cooked and diced

4 large oranges, peeled and segmented

150ml (5fl oz) mayonnaise

75g (3oz) almonds, toasted

Small pinch salt

1 lettuce, Cos-type

Small carton cress

Few sprigs of fresh mint, chopped

Mix together the diced potatoes, orange segments, mayonnaise, toasted almonds and salt.

Arrange the lettuce leaves round a suitable salad bowl, so that they form a lining. Into the centre of this, pour the potato mixture. Garnish with cress and chopped mint. Chill well before serving.

New potatoes. Serves 4.

A basically simple salad using natural produce from the Portuguese countryside.

Potato salad ring

England

2kg (4¼ lb) potatoes, cooked and peeled

175g (6oz) onions, peeled and grated

2 level tsp salt

Good grinding black pepper

2 tbsp parsley, chopped

275ml (10fl oz) water

25g (1oz) powdered gelatine

150ml (5fl oz) milk

275ml (10fl oz) mayonnaise

275ml (10fl oz) natural yogurt

1 level tsp English mustard

Cucumber, finely sliced for garnish

These quantities are sufficient for two 1.5 lt (2½ pt) moulds.

Brush the ring moulds with oil. Slice the potatoes and add them with the grated onions in layers into the moulds, seasoning each layer with salt, pepper and a sprinkling of chopped parsley.

Pour 150ml (5fl oz) of the water into a small container and sprinkle the gelatine over it. Leave until swollen and spongy. Heat the remaining water in a saucepan. Remove from the heat and stir in the soaked gelatine. Stir until dissolved. Allow to cool but not to set. When quite cool, add the milk, mayonnaise, yogurt and mustard and combine until smooth. Carefully pour this mixture over the potatoes and chill until well set.

Turn out on to a suitable serving dish and garnish with thinly sliced cucumber.

Waxy or new potatoes. Serves 12.

This is a most unusual salad but very simple to make.

Potato and white radish salad

India

1 crisp lettuce

450g (1 lb) potatoes, peeled, boiled and diced

225g (8oz) white radish, diced

225g (8oz) cauliflower florets

2 small green chillies, deseeded and chopped

175g (6oz) carrots, diced

2 tbsp coriander or parsley, chopped

1 tsp cumin powder

Salt and pepper to taste

2 tbsp cider vinegar

1 tsp raw cane sugar

Prepare all the vegetables and refrigerate for one hour, or until ready to serve.

Mix the cumin powder, salt, pepper, vinegar and sugar. Pour over the vegetables and herbs and stir carefully to coat.

Waxy or new potatoes. Serves 6. Vegetarian dish.

A spicy but delicious salad recipe, which can be served either as a side salad, or as an accompaniment to any selection of cold meats.

Potato, broad bean and yogurt salad   *Morocco*

450g (1 lb) potatoes, cooked
   and diced
1 small onion, finely diced
175g (6oz) broad beans,
   cooked
25g (1oz) crystallised ginger,
   finely chopped
110g (4oz) gherkin, chopped
150ml (5fl oz) yogurt, plain
1 tsp made French mustard
1 tbsp Muscovado sugar
Good pinch salt
2 tbsp parsley, chopped for
   garnish

Mix the diced potatoes, onion, broad beans, ginger and gherkin together. Stir together the yogurt, French mustard, sugar and salt. Pour this over the vegetables and combine carefully, coating all pieces.

Put into a suitable serving dish and garnish with chopped parsley.

Waxy or new potatoes. Serves 6. Vegetarian dish.

Bean curd and cooked vegetable salad   *Indonesia*

2 tbsp groundnut oil
2 red chillies, de-seeded
   and chopped
2 garlic cloves, crushed
110g (4oz) peanut butter
225ml (8fl oz) thick coconut
   milk
2 tbsp tamari sauce
½ tsp Laos powder, or pinch
   each ground ginger and
   black pepper
2 curry leaves, optional
1 tsp lemon juice
*For coconut milk use creamed
coconut block and water or milk*

350g (12oz) bean curd, (tofu)
Oil for deep-drying
350g (12oz) potatoes
225g (8oz) French beans
225g (8oz) Chinese cabbage
225g (8oz) carrots
½ cucumber

Dressing: fry the chillies and garlic for about 2 minutes in a little hot oil. Reduce to a fine paste in an electric blender or food processor. Add the peanut butter, coconut milk and tamari sauce and blend well. Put the mixture into a saucepan, add the Laos powder and curry leaves and bring to the boil. Allow to simmer gently until the sauce thickens a little. It should not be too thick and can be reduced by adding some water. Remove from the heat and stir in the lemon juice. Allow to cool.

Salad: divide the bean curd into about 1cm (½in) cubes and deep fry in hot oil, 350°F (180°C), until golden brown. Dry off excess oil from the curd by placing on an absorbent sheet of kitchen paper and allow to cool.

Boil the potatoes in their skins until just cooked. Skin and cut into cubes, allow to cool.

Top and tail the beans. Slice into pieces about 2.5cm (1in) long. Blanch in boiling water for 2 minutes, drain and plunge into cold water. When cold, drain. Finely shred the cabbage, blanch and cool as for beans for about 1 minute. Slice the carrots, blanch and cool for about 3 minutes.

Place the bean curd in the centre of a large serving dish. Carefully arrange the other vegetables in an attractive pattern around the curd.

Pour a little of the dressing over the salad and serve the remainder separately.

Waxy or new potatoes. Serves 6. Vegetarian dish.

Danish potato and herring salad   *Denmark*

(*see above*)

350g (12oz) potatoes
6 tbsp French dressing
5 rollmop herrings
3 medium-sized red skinned
    eating apples
6 sprigs cauliflower,
    blanched
6 brussels sprouts, cooked
Juice and zest of 1 lemon
Salt and freshly ground black
    pepper
Lettuce leaves

Peel and boil the potatoes in salted water until just tender. Drain thoroughly and dice. While still warm pour over the French dressing and stir carefully to coat the potatoes. Set side to cool. Cut the rollmops into 2.5cm (1in) pieces. Core the apples with the skins on and cut into slices.

Combine the rollmops, apples, cauliflower and sprouts with the dressed potatoes, adding the lemon juice and zest at the same time and season to taste.

Line a suitable dish with the lettuce leaves and pile the mixture on top. Cover and chill for at least 1 hour before serving.

Waxy or new potatoes. Serves 6.

Creole potato salad

(see page 17 for illustration)

USA

450g (1 lb) potatoes, boiled
and sliced

275ml (10fl oz) whole prawns,
cooked and peeled

6 tbsp French dressing,
warmed

1 lettuce, green, Iceberg

1 lettuce, red, Radicchio

2 medium eggs, hard boiled
and shelled

2 chilli peppers, deseeded
and diced

Black pepper to.taste

Mix together the sliced potatoes and prawns. Pour the French dressing over the mixture.

Arrange on a bed of lettuce and garnish with slices of hard boiled egg, diced chillies and ground black pepper.

Waxy or new potatoes. Serves 4.

Creole cookery is a most interesting blend of the best of Spanish and French cuisine. Traditional recipes have been subtly adapted and added to try the exotic cooks of New Orleans.

Potato salad with rollmops

Germany

2 medium potatoes, boiled in
their skins

2 tbsp olive oil

1 tbsp wine vinegar

1 large gherkin, sliced

Salt and pepper to taste

4 rollmop herrings

1 tbsp parsley, chopped

Peel and slice the potatoes while still warm. Mix the olive oil, wine vinegar, salt and pepper and pour over the warm potatoes.

Arrange the rollmops on top of the potato mixture and garnish with chopped parsley.

Waxy or new potatoes. Serves 4.

German cooking is delicious but essentially homely, and catering for hearty appetites.

Potato and tomato salad with anchovies

Portugal

6 medium potatoes, cooked
and sliced

6 large tomatoes, peeled and
sliced

2 tbsp olive or salad oil

1 tbsp wine vinegar

1 tsp tarragon vinegar

1 tbsp shallot or spring
onions, chopped

1 tsp sugar

Salt and pepper to taste

Small tin of anchovies,
drained and chopped

A few olives, if desired

Arrange alternate slices of potatoes and tomatoes in a salad bowl. Mix together the oil, vinegars, shallots or spring onions, sugar, seasoning, chopped anchovies and olives.

Pour the mixture over the potatoes and tomatoes. Chill well before serving.

Waxy or new potatoes. Serves 6.

Mussels with potatoes (Mejillones con patata)   *Spain*
(see above)

450g (1 lb) mussels, cooked and shelled

225g (8oz) potatoes, cooked and diced

175g (6oz) carrots, cooked and diced

1 tbsp olive oil

3 tbsp wine vinegar

Salt and freshly ground black pepper to season

Mix together the mussels, potatoes and carrots and arrange on a suitable serving dish.

Thoroughly blend the oil, vinegar and seasoning and pour over the salad. Chill well before serving.

Waxy or new potatoes. Serves 4.

An unusual hors d'oeuvre but one typical of Northern Spain. By increasing the quantity of mussels, I sometimes serve this as a main luncheon dish, accompanied by fresh, crusty bread with butter.

Potato, kiwi and fish salad

New Zealand

(see opposite)

1 medium cucumber, sliced
450g (1 lb) potatoes, boiled
    in their skins
3 kiwi fruit, skinned and
    sliced
225g (8oz) tin salmon
1 tbsp mayonnaise
110g (4oz) prawns, cooked
    and peeled
1 small onion, chopped
1 small apple, green, diced
Salt and pepper
Parsley for garnish

Arrange the cucumber slices round the edge of a large plate. Slice the potatoes as evenly as posible and arrange on the inside of the cucumber. Similarly arrange the kiwi fruit on the inside of the potatoes.

Mash the tinned salmon with the mayonnaise. Mix in the prawns, onion, apple, salt and pepper and arrange this in a pile in the middle of the salad. Garnish with the parsley.

Waxy or new potatoes. Serves 4.

Potato and white fish salad

Denmark

700g (1½ lb) fillets white fish
225g (8oz) potatoes, cooked
Small bunch spring onions,
    finely chopped
1 tbsp fresh parsley, chopped
10g (½oz) ground coriander
Salt and freshly ground black
    pepper
1 tbsp olive oil
2 tbsp wine vinegar
1 tsp sugar
*Use bass, cod, haddock, hake,
halibut, sole, turbot for this dish.*

Steam the fish, or gently poach in boiling water for 10 minutes, or until cooked. Drain, skin and remove any bones. Break into coarse pieces.

While still warm, dice the cooked potatoes. Put a layer of potatoes in a suitable salad bowl, top with a layer of fish, then a sprinkling of onion, parsley, coriander, salt and pepper. Repeat the layers once more.

Mix the olive oil, wine vinegar and sugar thoroughly and pour over the mixture. Chill for at least 4 hours before serving.

Waxy or new potatoes. Serves 6.

Delano salad

Italy

450g (1 lb) potatoes
450g (1 lb) rare beef
450g (1 lb) tomatoes, skinned
    and de-seeded
225g (8oz) French beans,
    cooked
1 medium egg, hard-boiled
150ml (5fl oz) vinaigrette
1 tbsp parsley, finely chopped
1 tbsp chives, finely chopped

Cook the potatoes, leaving the skins on if new potatoes, until tender. Drain and allow to cool. Cut the beef and tomatoes into thin strips. Slice the cold potatoes.

Arrange the French beans around the edge of a serving dish, with the sliced potatoes in the middle and overlapping the beans. Place strips of beef on top of the potatoes and the tomatoes on top of the beans. Sieve the egg yolk over the beef and sprinkle the finely chopped white over the tomatoes.

Combine the vinaigrette dressing with the parsley and chives. Pour over the salad and chill well before serving. Serve with fresh, crusty bread and butter.

Waxy or new potatoes. Serves 4.

Soups

Soup became part of our diet way back in the mists of history, probably around the time that the first crude clay cooking pots were developed. Meat, fish, grasses or grains were placed in these pots and water poured over them, much as we still do today. The dish was then simmered over an open fire until the ingredients were tender. The solids were removed and eaten but, when very hungry, early man supped the remaining broth and discovered how delicious it was. It is possible that the word 'soup' has been derived from 'sup' and this nourishing dish has remained a basic part of our diet for many centuries.

As the idea of using a liquid as a food spread from one country to another, imaginative cooks added their own variations, depending mainly on what was available. Different countries developed their own traditional dishes, such as the famous recipes for Borscht (Russia and Poland), Cock-a-leekie (Scotland), Gazpacho (Spain), and Bouillabaisse (France).

Soup is easy to prepare and cook and is fairly kind to the family budget. The use of a pressure cooker cuts down the cooking time. It is also a most comforting food, especially the thick, rib-sticking variety served on a cold winter's night. Potato soup of any variety is perfect for this purpose, served either as a warming luncheon or supper dish. It is always best to make any soup on the thick side, as it can easily be thinned down if necessary by adding more stock, cream or milk. It is also a marvellous way of using up all the small, misshapen and damaged vegetables that might otherwise be discarded.

The most simple soup can be turned into a gastronomic delight by the addition of a suitable garnish. Try sprinkling a little chopped parsley or chives and paprika or, for something different, finely sieved hard-boiled egg yolk over a light-coloured soup. Dark-coloured soups need a contrast such as a sprinkling of grated cheese, or hard-boiled egg white finely chopped. Try adding a swirl of fresh cream to the surface of a cold soup.

Opposite: see page 39 for
Chilled potato and saffron soup recipe.

Potato soup *Australia*

225g (8oz) potatoes, diced
2 stalks celery, diced
1 large onion, diced
¼ tsp salt
425ml (15fl oz) water
2 tbsp parsley, finely chopped
275ml (10fl oz) milk

Put all ingredients except the parsley and milk in a saucepan. Bring to the boil and simmer gently for 1 hour. Add the parsley and milk just before serving and re-heat but do not boil.

Waxy potatoes. Serves 4. Vegetarian dish.

Grated potato soup (Sopa de patata rallada) *Spain*

1½ lt (3 pt) potato stock,
  (see page 140)
700g (1½ lb) potatoes
Salt and pepper to taste
1 medium egg, hard-boiled
1 tbsp parsley, chopped

Bring the stock to the boil, grate the potatoes and add to the stock and season. Cook for 15 minutes. Serve garnished with grated hard-boiled egg and chopped parsley.

Waxy potatoes. Serves 6.

This soup is easy to prepare and ideal for unexpected guests.

Potato soup with butter and parsley *Finland*

350g (12oz) cooked mashed
  potatoes
425ml (15fl oz) milk
275ml (10fl oz) half milk and
  water mixed
1 tsp salt
Good grinding black pepper
Good pinch of ground
  allspice
2 tbsp fresh parsley, finely
  chopped
50g (2oz) butter

In a large saucepan beat the mashed potatoes and milk with a whisk until smooth, or rub through a sieve if preferred. Stir in the half milk and half water and heat until almost boiling. Add salt and pepper, noting that you can use white pepper if you do not like the speckles of black, and stir in the allspice. Serve very hot, sprinkle with the chopped parsley and a few flakes of butter.

Floury potatoes. Serves 6. Vegetarian dish.

This is a lovely way to use up left-over potatoes from the previous night's dinner.

Potato and chervil soup *England*

50g (2oz) butter
700g (1½ lb) potatoes, peeled
  and sliced
1 large onion, chopped
900ml (1½ pt) chicken stock
½ tsp grated nutmeg
Salt and fresh ground black
  pepper
150ml (5fl oz) single cream, or
  top of the milk
6 tbsp fresh chervil, chopped
Croutons for garnish

Heat the butter and sweat the potatoes and onion very gently in a covered saucepan, stirring occasionally for 5 to 6 minutes. Pour in the chicken stock. Add the nutmeg and seasonings and bring to boiling point. Turn the heat down and allow to simmer for 20 to 25 minutes. Liquidise the soup or pass through a sieve and return to the saucepan. Stir in the cream and chopped chervil and heat through. Serve garnished with the croutons.

Floury potatoes. Serves 6.

The use of fresh chervil is really essential to the flavour of this soup.

Chilled potato and saffron soup with herbs *Belgium*

(see page 37 for illustration)

3 large onions
2 large potatoes
25g (1oz) butter
1 chicken stock cube
500ml (18fl oz) milk
150ml (5fl oz) dry white wine
¼ tsp saffron powder
Salt and freshly ground
    pepper to taste
55ml (2fl oz) double cream
2 tsp freshly chopped herbs,
    parsley, chives and
    tarragon
55ml (2fl oz) sour cream

To sour cream, add 1 tsp lime or lemon juice to every 150ml (5fl oz) cream. Leave for 30 minutes before use.

Peel and chop the onions. Peel and dice the potatoes. Slowly melt the butter in a heavy-bottomed pan and fry the onions until transparent. Add the potatoes and stir for about 3 minutes.

In a separate pan, dissolve the stock cube in the milk and wine and bring almost to boiling point. Add the saffron powder and mix well with the onions and potatoes.

Gently simmer for 30 minutes then liquidise to a purée. Return to the pan and season. Stir in the cream. Cover and chill thoroughly. Serve topped with freshly chopped herbs and a swirl of sour cream.

Floury potatoes. Serves 4. Substitute the chicken stock cube for a vegetarian dish.

This is a good recipe for freezing. It is delicious served well-chilled with some fresh, crusty bread.

Light potato soup (Lichte Kartoffelsuppe) *Austria*

450g (1 lb) potatoes
1 large carrot
1 parsnip
1 stick celery
1 onion
Good pinch of thyme
1 dsp flour
275ml (10fl oz) milk
10g (½oz) butter
1 tbsp parsley, chopped

Peel and dice the potatoes, carrot and parsnip and cut the celery and onion into small pieces. Put all into a large saucepan, cover with water, sprinkle in the thyme and bring to the boil. Allow to cook for about 40 minutes, then liquidise or pass through a sieve.

Mix the flour to a smooth paste with a little of the milk and stir into the sieved vegetables. Add the butter, the remainder of the milk and heat and cook for 3 minutes. Serve garnished with the chopped parsley.

Waxy potatoes. Serves 4. Vegetarian dish.

Austrian soups are generally healthy and filling and can easily be transformed into a main meal with typically Austrian additions; for example, Frankfurters cut into small pieces can be used.

Spiced potato soup *Malaysia*

1 large onion, chopped
75g (3oz) butter
1.15 lt (2 pt) milk
2 large potatoes, peeled,
    boiled and diced
75g (3oz) plain flour
1 tsp curry powder
Salt and peper to taste
½ tsp celery salt
2 tbsp parsley, chopped

Fry the onion in the butter until soft but not brown. Add the milk and bring to just under the boil. Very carefully whisk the hot milk and onions into the potatoes. Add the flour, curry powder, salt, pepper and celery salt.

Bring back to just under the boil and simmer gently for 5 minutes. Pass through a strainer or liquidise. Serve very hot garnished with the chopped parsley.

Floury potatoes. Serves 6. Vegetarian dish.

Leek and potato soup

Mexico

(see above)

1 tbsp cooking oil

½ onion, finely chopped or grated

2 large potatoes

2 large leeks

2 tbsp parsley, chopped

2 tbsp tomato purée

½ tsp salt

Good grinding of black pepper

900ml (1½ pt) warmed Chicken stock

Heat the oil in a large saucepan and gently fry the onion until soft and clear but not browned. Peel and dice the potatoes. Carefully wash the leeks and slice finely. Add the potatoes, leeks, parsley, tomato purée, and seasonings to the onion, stir in the oil for a few minutes, then carefully pour the chicken stock over. Bring to a gentle simmer and allow to cook for approximately 15 minutes, until the potato is cooked.

Waxy or new potatoes. Serves 6. Substitute the chicken stock for a vegetarian dish.

The addition of tomato purée gives a warm colour to this soup. It is a simple soup to make, yet one that is full of nourishment and a great favourite with all my guests.

Swiss style potato soup

Switzerland

1 large onion, chopped
50g (2oz) butter
450g (1 lb) potatoes, peeled and diced
225g (8oz) turnip, peeled and diced
40g (1½oz) plain flour
600ml (1 pt) boiling potato stock (see page 140)
600ml (1 pt) milk, very hot
Good pinch mace or nutmeg
Salt and pepper to taste
25g (1oz) butter

Fry the chopped onion in butter until soft but not browned. Add the diced potatoes and turnip. Put in the flour and stir well. Slowly add the stock, milk and mace and season to taste.

Bring to a simmer and cook gently for 20 minutes. Pass through a sieve or liquidise. Serve garnished with flakes of butter scattered on top.

Floury potatoes. Serves 8. Vegetarian dish.

Minted potato soup with croutons

Belgium

900g (2 lb) small new potatoes
50g (2oz) butter
900ml (1½ pt) milk
3 tbsp fresh mint
1 tbsp fresh parsley
Salt and pepper to taste

Wash the potatoes but do not peel. Melt the butter in a large saucepan. Add potatoes and stir to coat with the butter. Pour in the milk, add the herbs and season to taste. Bring to a gentle simmer and cook for 20 minutes, or until the potatoes are tender, topping up with milk if necessary. Serve piping hot and garnish with croutons.

New potatoes. Serves 6. Vegetarian dish.

Tattie hushie

England

700g (1½ lb) potatoes, peeled and diced
1 large leek, thinly sliced
50g (2oz) butter
25g (2oz) medium coarse oatmeal
1.15 lt (2 pt) skimmed milk
2 tsp salt
Good grinding black pepper
1 tbsp tomato sauce or ketchup

Cook the potatoes in water until almost tender. Add the leek and cook for a further 5 minutes. Drain and mash thoroughly with the butter. Mix in the oatmeal, milk and seasonings. Stirring constantly, gently bring to just below boiling point. Serve with a swirl of the tomato sauce.

Floury potatoes. Serves 6. Vegetarian dish.

This Scottish sounding soup is actually from the English border country.

Crème du Barry

France

225g (8oz) potatoes
450g (1 lb) cauliflower florets
900ml (1½ pt) water
½ tsp grated nutmeg
425ml (15fl oz) milk
Salt and freshly ground black pepper
25g (1oz) butter
Croutons for garnish

Peel and dice potatoes and put in a large saucepan. Add the cauliflower florets and water. Cover, bring to a simmer and cook for 30 minutes. Liquidise or rub through a sieve.

Return to saucepan and add the nutmeg, milk, salt, pepper and butter. Reheat thoroughly and serve garnished with croutons, cubes of toasted or deep fried bread.

Floury potatoes. Serves 6. Vegetarian dish.

Potato and kale soup (Caldo verde)   *Portugal*

450g (1 lb) potatoes, peeled and sliced

1 large onion, peeled and chopped

225g (8oz) kale, destalked and sliced

Salt and freshly grounded black pepper

4 tbsp olive oil

Place the sliced potatoes in a large saucepan and cover with cold water. Bring to the boil and simmer until cooked. Either liquidise the potatoes or pass all through a sieve. Return to the saucepan and add sufficient water to make a thin liquid. Bring back to the boil and add the chopped onion and sliced kale. Season to taste, noting that the soup should be 'peppery'. Allow to simmer for 15 minutes. Serve in soup bowls and pour a tablespoon of olive oil on top of each serving.

Floury potatoes. Serves 4. Vegetarian dish.

Almost every Portuguese restaurant serves its own version of this simple but wonderfully warming soup. It can be served as a main course dish with some crusty bread and cheese.

Green soup   *India*

5 medium potatoes, peeled and diced

1 large onion, peeled and chopped

110g (4oz) kale leaves, coarsely chopped

4 large cloves of garlic, peeled and chopped

1½ tsp salt

1 lt (2½ pt) water

1 tbsp good olive oil

Good grinding black pepper

In a large saucepan put the potatoes, onion, kale, garlic and salt. Pour in the water and bring to the boil. Cover, lower the heat and simmer gently for about 1 hour. Either blend with an electric mixer or pass through a sieve so that you have a smooth, creamy liquid.

Return to the saucepan, check the seasoning and add more water if too thick. Just before serving add the olive oil and black pepper.

Floury potatoes. Serves 8. Vegetarian dish.

This is a thick and hearty soup, not unlike the better known leek and potato version or the similar Portuguese soup.

Winter soup from Devon   *England*

50g (2oz) butter

3 large leeks, chopped

1 large onion, chopped

2 large carrots, grated

450g (1 lb) potatoes, peeled and diced

1 lt (1¾ pt) chicken stock

Salt and freshly ground black pepper

275ml (10fl oz) milk

2 tbsp parsley, chopped

150ml (5fl oz) double cream

A few peeled prawns and cooked mussels

Good pinch paprika

Melt the butter in a large, heavy saucepan. Add the leeks, onion, carrots and potatoes and cook gently, stirring constantly to avoid sticking, for about 8 minutes. Pour in the stock, season and continue to simmer for 20 minutes until the vegetables are soft.

Liquidize the soup, or pass through a sieve. Return to pan and bring slowly back to a simmer. Add the milk, parsley, cream, prawns and mussels and heat, but do not allow to boil. Serve garnished with a good pinch of paprika.

Floury potatoes. Serves 6.

Crécy soup

France

50g (2oz) butter
225g (8oz) potatoes, peeled and diced
225g (8oz) carrots, peeled and sliced
1 medium onion, chopped
2 stalks celery, sliced
1 clove garlic, crushed
600ml (1 pt) potato stock, (see page 140)
Salt and pepper to taste
150ml (5fl oz) milk
1 carrot, finely grated for garnish

Melt butter and fry the potato, carrots, onion, celery and garlic stirring continuously for 3 minutes. Add the stock and allow to simmer for 25 minutes. Pass through a sieve or liquidise. Season with salt and pepper, add the milk and bring to just below boiling point but do not boil. Serve garnished with the finely grated carrot.

Floury potatoes. Serves 8. Vegetarian dish.

I sometimes heat the grated carrot with a little butter in a saucepan and then stir into the creamed soup to add texture as well as colour and garnish.

Curried vegetable soup

Indonesia

½ tsp ground turmeric
¼ tsp Laos powder
1 garlic clove crushed
1 medium onion, grated
2 tbsp groundnut oil
225g (8oz) potatoes
225g (8oz) carrots
110g (4oz) green cabbage
1 green pepper
110g (4oz) shelled green peas
425ml (15fl oz) medium-thick coconut milk
425ml (15fl oz) vegetable stock
2 curry leaves, chopped (optional)
1 stalk lemon balm, chopped

Put the turmeric, Laos powder or equivalent, garlic, onion and 1 tbsp of oil into an electric blender or food processor amd blend to a smooth paste. Peel and dice the potatoes. Thinly slice the carrots. Shred the cabbage. Core, deseed and dice the pepper.

Heat the remaining oil in a wok or large frying pan over a medium heat. Add the spice and onion paste and stir-fry for 2 minutes or until it cleanly leaves the sides of the pan. Add the coconut milk and stock and bring all to the boil. Add the vegetables, curry leaves if required, and lemon balm. Simmer uncovered until the vegetables are tender but not over cooked.

Waxy potatoes. Serves 6. Vegetarian dish.

If Laos powder is not available, I use a pinch each of ground ginger and black pepper.

Tomato, potato and onion soup

Spain

(Sopa de tomate, patata y cebolla)

4 medium tomatoes, peeled and chopped
1 large onion, chopped
2 tbsp olive oil
700g (1½ lb) potatoes, peeled and sliced
1½ lt (3 pt) potato stock, (see page 140)
Salt and pepper to taste
2 medium egg yolks, beaten
Fried bread croutons

Fry the tomatoes and onion gently in the olive oil, add the sliced potatoes, stock and seasonings and simmer for 1 hour. Liquidise or pass through a sieve.

Beating constantly, add the egg yolks by dribbling in a little at a time. Return to heat but do not allow to boil. Serve with the croutons floating on top.

Floury potatoes. Serves 6.

This makes a substantial soup and the egg 'threads' add an interesting texture.

Watercress soup (Soupe au cresson) *France*

450g (1 lb) potatoes
1 lt (1¾ pt) cold potato stock (see page 140) or water
2 bunches watercress
Salt and freshly ground black pepper
2 tbsp double cream
1 tbsp parsley, chopped

Peel and cut potatoes into small pieces. Boil in the stock until well cooked. Rinse the watercress thoroughly and chop it all, including the stalks, finely but keep a few leaves for garnish. Add to the potatoes and increase heat for 3 minutes. Season with salt and pepper and strain the soup through a Mouli-Legume. Re-heat but do not boil.

Just before serving carefully stir in the cream, sprinkle with the parsley and garnish with the watercress leaves.

Floury potatoes. Serves 6. Vegetarian dish.

This classic, well-known soup, has a fresh and piquant flavour.

Cream of potato soup with brussels sprouts and bacon *Holland*

(see below)

225g (8oz) potatoes, peeled and grated
700g (1½ lb) brussels sprouts or sprout tops, chopped
1 large onion, chopped
2 medium cloves of garlic, crushed
110g (4oz) butter
900ml (1½ pt) stock
275ml (10fl oz) milk
Good pinch ground nutmeg
Good pinch mustard powder
Salt and freshly ground black pepper
4 rashers streaky bacon, grilled until crisp
2 tbsp chopped chives or spring onion
50g (2oz) grated cheese

Put all ingredients except bacon, chives and cheese into a large saucepan and bring slowly to just below boiling point, cover and allow to simmer for 40 minutes. Remove from the heat and liquidise or rub through a sieve.

Return to heat and bring back to a simmer. Serve topped with crumbled pieces of bacon, chopped chives and grated cheese.

Floury potatoes. Serves 8.

Mulligatawny soup

India

50g (2oz) butter
225g (8oz) potatoes, peeled
  and diced
1 small onion, chopped
1 large carrot, diced
1 large cooking apple, peeled
  and sliced
40g (1½oz) curry powder
2 tsp tomato purée
600ml (1 pt) good beef stock
1 lime, grated rind and juice
Salt and black pepper

Melt the butter and fry the potatoes, onion, carrot, apple, curry powder and tomato purée for about 8 minutes, stirring continuously. Add the beef stock and juice of the lime and reheat. Season with salt and pepper to taste. Serve very hot with the grated lime rind scattered on top.

Waxy potatoes. Serves 6.

I have made this soup many times as it is hearty and warming on a cold day. However, one Indian friend strongly denies that apple should be used. The choice is yours!

Ham, egg and potato soup

Spain

(Sopa de patata, con jamon y huevo)

1.8 lt (3 pt) chicken stock
4 medium potatoes, peeled
  and mashed
2 medium eggs, hard-boiled
110g (4oz) ham, chopped
Salt and pepper to taste
1 tbsp parsley, chopped

Heat the stock to boiling point. Add the potatoes. Grate the hard-boiled eggs and add to the soup with the ham. Season and serve garnished with a sprinkling of chopped parsley.

Floury potatoes. Serves 6.

Jean Ross's potato and hambone soup

Scotland

(see front cover for illustration)

4 large ham bones
450g (1 lb) potatoes, peeled
  and sliced
450g (1 lb) carrots, peeled
  and grated
225g (8oz) onions, peeled
  and chopped
110g (4oz) swede, peeled
  and grated
2 tbsp parsley
1 tbsp parsley for garnish

Make a good stock with the ham bones. Strain and allow to cool. Skim off any surplus fat. Add all the vegetables and cook at simmering point for about 45 minutes. Stir in the 1 tbsp parsley and serve piping hot.

Waxy potatoes. Serves 6.

Jean Ross is my mum and she makes the best soups I have ever tasted! It is perhaps a little difficult to obtain ham bones nowadays but this soup can be made with a ham hock or an end piece. The meat could then be taken off and cut into small pieces and served in the soup.

Soup with potato balls (Sopa de bolitas)

Spain

110g (4oz) ham, chopped
75g (3oz) butter
700g (1½ lb) potatoes, peeled,
  boiled and sieved
Salt and pepper to taste
1 medium egg, beaten
Olive oil, or vegetable oil
1.8 lt (3 pt) chicken stock

Fry the ham in the butter which has been allowed to brown slightly. Beat this into the sieved potatoes and season to taste. Mix in the beaten egg. Make into walnut sized pieces and roll into round balls.

Heat some oil in a frying pan, or chip pan, and cook the potato balls gently, taking care not to break them. Drain on kitchen paper. Bring the stock to simmering point and drop the balls into it. Serve at once.

Floury potatoes. Serves 6.

Goulash soup with potatoes (Gulaschsuppe)   *Austria*

110g (4oz) streaky bacon
1 medium onion, chopped
225g (8oz) braising steak, diced
2 tsp paprika
¼ tsp marjoram
1 clove garlic, crushed
50g (2oz) plain flour
1.15 lt (2 pt) beef stock
2 large potatoes, cooked and diced

Chop bacon and gently fry with the chopped onion. When a nice golden colour, add the diced steak and allow to brown all over, stirring constantly. Gradually stir in the paprika, marjoram and crushed garlic. Take off the heat and add the flour. Stir thoroughly and then slowly stir in the stock.

Return to heat and bring to a gentle simmer. Cook on simmer for 30 minutes. Now add the diced potato and heat through.

Waxy potatoes. Serves 6.

This is one of the many recipes from the soup loving Austrian monks who sometimes had to suffer a penance of only one portion of soup per day.

Fish soup (Chourbat)   *Tunisia*

700g (1½ lb) firm fleshed white fish
110g (4oz) onions, chopped
110g (4oz) celery, chopped
110g (4oz) potatoes, diced
50g (2oz) butter
225g (8oz) tomatoes, peeled and chopped
1 lt (1¾ pt) fish stock, or water
4 medium cloves of garlic, crushed
3 tbsp parsley, chopped
Salt and pepper to taste
110g (4oz) soup noodles

Skin the fish and remove any bones. Cut into about 2.5cm (1in) pieces. Fry the onions, celery and potatoes in the butter for 5 minutes. Add the tomatoes and allow to cook slowly for another 5 minutes. Pour on the fish stock or water and season.

Add the fish pieces, crushed garlic and the chopped parsley and season to taste. Cook at a gentle simmer for 10 minutes. Remove the fish from the liquid but keep warm, then add the noodles to the soup and continue simmering for a further 10 minutes. Serve the soup in bowls with the fish on a side dish.

Waxy potatoes. Serves 6.

Traditionally in Tunisia the chourbat contains several types of fish such as grouper, congereel, hogfish and red gurnard. As these are not all readily available internationally I have suggested the substitution of a firm fleshed white fish.

Oyster soup   *Ireland*

3 large potatoes, peeled
1 lt (1¾ pt) boiling milk
Bouquet garni
Good grinding of pepper
36 fresh oysters
175g (6oz) belly of pork
1 tsp salt
50g (2oz) butter

Cook the potatoes in boiling salted water until tender. Drain, then mash and add the milk, bouquet garni and season to taste. In the meantime, open the oysters and reserve their juices.

Dice the belly of pork and fry gently until just cooked. Add the pork, oysters and their juices to the potatoes and milk and bring almost to boiling point. Gently simmer for 5 minutes, add the butter and serve.

Floury potatoes. Serves 4.

Fish and potato soup with tomato

Mexico

(see below)

450g (1 lb) fish heads, tails, bones and trimmings

1 large onion

1 bay leaf

½ tsp salt

Good grinding of black pepper

1 large potato, peeled and diced, reserve the skin

900ml (1½ pt) chicken stock

2 tbsp parsley, chopped

2 tbsp tomato purée

25g (1oz) fresh or frozen peas

10 stuffed olives

110g (4oz) fillet of fish, skinned and boned

Parsley for garnish

1 lemon, sliced

Put fish trimmings, onion, bay leaf, salt, pepper and potato skin into a large saucepan containing the chicken stock. Bring to the boil and gently simmer for approximately 30 minutes. Strain the liquid off into a clean saucepan and add diced potato, parsley, tomato puree, peas and olives. Cut fillet of fish into 2.5cm (1in) pieces and add to liquid. Cook on a very low heat for 10 minutes. Serve very hot garnished with a little more parsley and the lemon slices.

Waxy potatoes. Serves 6.

Served with fresh crusty bread this soup can make a substantial lunch on a cold day.

Classic recipes and side dishes

In this section I have tried to give a wide variety of potato dishes that are almost universally known either as a garnish, a side dish or, as in the case of the humble Potatoes à la paysanne (Pommes de terre à la paysanne), as a main course if served with a crisp green salad and some fresh crusty bread. I have mentioned that Potatoes à la paysanne can be extended to a main course but so, too, can many of the other recipes. Try serving some of them with a dish of hot buttered cabbage or swede, or some whole baked onions.

It is a common error to assume that potatoes are a cheap meal, although it is true that even today they are relatively inexpensive. Because of the way they combine and blend with other ingredients and by adding small quantities of other exotic foods, a simple dish can be transformed into a gourmet's delight.

I think one of the most renowned French potato dishes is Aligot, which comes from the Auvergne region of France. The French housewife is praised for her housekeeping and sound economical habits and this simple recipe can be eaten on its own as a luncheon or supper dish but it is also ideal served with grilled meats.

Some of these recipes can also be adapted and used as savoury snacks to serve with drinks. I would particularly recommend serving a dish of hot Château potatoes speared with cocktail sticks but be careful not to serve them too hot. However, if you really want something special and different to serve with your drinks, try the recipe for Milanese croquettes but do make them smaller than stated, say, large marble size. Again, serve hot garnished with parsley and speared with cocktail sticks.

I have entitled this section 'Classic recipes and side dishes' but the two are easily interchangeable. By the term 'Classic', I mean the long-established methods of cooking the potatoes and with a little ingenuity, these can be adapted to make interesting side dishes, or accompaniments to a main course.

Opposite: see page 55 for Château potatoes recipe and page 57 for Duchess potatoes.

Chips *Scotland*

900g (2 lb) potatoes, peeled
Oil or fat for deep frying
Salt

Cut the potatoes into fingers about 1cm (½in) square by 5cm (2in) long. Wash and dry off on a clean tea towel.

Place in a chip basket and cook in hot fat until tender, without colouring.

Remove from the fat and drain. Plunge again into the hot fat and allow to colour to an even golden brown. Sprinkle with salt and serve.

Floury or waxy potatoes. Serves 6. Vegetarian dish.

Soufflé potatoes (Pommes de terre soufflées) *France*

450g (1 lb) potatoes of even
size
Fat for deep frying
Salt to taste

Peel, trim and cut the potatoes into even slices about 3mm (⅛in) thick. Rinse in cold water, then dry on a clean tea cloth.

Gradually heat the fat to a medium heat and fry the slices until they begin to rise in the fat. Remove and drain in a frying basket.

Bring the fat heat up again until hot and a blue haze can be seen. Plunge the potato slices in and cook until golden brown and puffed up. Drain on absorbent paper, sprinkle with salt and serve with drinks.

Floury potatoes. Serves 6. Vegetarian dish.

Sauté potatoes *France*

900g (2 lb) potatoes
25g (1oz) butter
1 tbsp olive oil
Salt and freshly ground black
pepper
1 tbsp parsley, chopped

Boil the potatoes in their skins for 15 minutes. Peel and cut into even slices.

Heat the butter and oil in a deep frying pan and when hot, add the sliced potatoes. Season with a little salt and cook until golden brown on both sides, shaking the pan occasionally to prevent sticking. Season to taste. Turn into a serving dish and garnish with chopped parsley.

Waxy, new or floury potatoes. Serves 6. Vegetarian dish.

To ensure that you have really crisp sauté potatoes use olive oil and, if possible, use more than one frying pan, so that the potatoes can cook in a single layer.

Parmentier potatoes *France*

(Pommes de terre Parmentier)

(see below)

700g (1½ lb) potatoes
225g (8oz) butter
1 tbsp parsley, chopped for garnish

Peel and cut the potatoes into small pieces, about 1cm (½in) square. Cook in melted butter. Sprinkle with the chopped parsley as garnish.

Alternatively, cook the potatoes around the meat with which they are to be served, until golden brown.

Waxy or floury potatoes. Serves 4. Vegetarian dish.

Potato croutons *Norway*

225g (8oz) potatoes, peeled and diced
600ml (1 pt) boiling, salted water
Oil or fat to deep fry
Salt

Run cold water through the diced potatoes to remove the starch. Drain and dry thoroughly. Blanch the potatoes in boiling, salted water for 2 minutes and again drain and dry thoroughly. Bring the oil or fat to a hot temperature where you can see a blue haze and fry the croutons until golden brown.

Drain on kitchen paper and sprinkle with salt.

Waxy potatoes. Serves 4. Vegetarian dish.

I have also used leftover cold cooked potatoes or the waxy variety to make croutons. This is a good way of using up left over potatoes from a previous meal. They are good to eat as a snack with drinks but better still for garnishing a bowl of hot home-made soup.

Darfin potatoes (Pommes de terre Darfin) _France_

900g (2 lb) potatoes
2 tbsp olive oil
175g (6oz) butter
Salt and pepper to taste

Peel the potatoes and cut into matchsticks. Place in a clean tea cloth and squeeze out as much moisture as possible. Heat a little oil and butter in a heavy frying pan. Put a handful of the potato matchsticks into the pan and flatten to make a small circular cake. Sprinkle lightly with salt and pepper and cook on both sides until well browned.

Carefully roll each cake into a cornet shape and keep warm until all the mixture has been cooked.

Waxy or floury potatoes. Serves 8. Vegetarian dish.

Chatouillard potatoes _France_
(Pommes frites Chatouillard)

700g (1½ lb) potatoes
Fat for deep frying

Peel the potatoes, then cut into ribbon strips by peeling off the flesh in a spiral fashion, about 3mm (⅛in) thick.

Gradually heat the fat to a medium heat and fry the strips until they start to rise in the fat. Remove and drain in a frying basket.

Bring the fat heat up again until hot and a blue haze can be seen. Plunge the potato strips in and cook until golden brown and puffed up. Drain on absorbent paper, sprinkle with salt and serve with drinks.

Waxy or floury potatoes. Serves 6. Vegetarian dish.

Rissole potatoes (Pommes de terre rissolées) _France_

900g (2 lb) small potatoes
2 tbsp butter
Salt and freshly ground black
 pepper
2 tbsp parsley, chopped
2 tbsp chives, chopped
2 spring onions, finely
 chopped

Boil the potatoes in their skins until tender but not soft. Drain and rinse thoroughly in cold water as this aids the easy removal of the skins.

Heat the butter in a large frying pan until it foams, add the potatoes and brown lightly. Cover, turn down heat and cook for 15 minutes. Remove the lid, increase the heat, shaking the pan so that the potatoes will be crisp on the outside. Serve immediately, sprinkled with salt, pepper, the herbs and the onions.

Waxy or new potatoes. Serves 4. Vegetarian dish.

Anna potatoes (Pommes de terre Anna) _France_

700g (1½ lb) potatoes
175g (6oz) butter
Salt and pepper to taste

Peel the potatoes as evenly as possible and thinly slice. Rinse in cold water and dry on a clean tea cloth. Season with salt and pepper.

Melt the butter and sauté the potato slices gently until they are impregnated with the butter. Make into a cake shape by pressing with a fork. Brown on one side, turn the cake over and brown on the other side.

Waxy potatoes. Serves 6. Vegetarian dish.

Potatoes with whole spices and sesame *India*

900g (2 lb) medium potatoes
2 tsp whole cumin seeds
¼ tsp whole fenugreek seeds
2 tsp whole black mustard
   seeds
6 tbsp vegetable oil
2 hot red peppers, de-seeded
2 tbsp sesame seeds
¼ tsp ground turmeric
1½ tsp salt
Good grinding of black
   pepper
2 tbsp lemon juice

Par-boil the potatoes in their jackets, drain and allow to cool for several hours. Peel the potatoes and dice.

Mix the cumin, fenugreek and mustard seeds in a small bowl. Place all the ingredients near the cooker and heat the oil in a large, heavy frying pan. When very hot, add the spices in this sequence; the combined cumin mixture and let them sizzle for about 5 seconds, the peppers stirring thoroughly for 3 seconds, then the sesame seeds and stir for a further 5 seconds. Stir in the turmeric and diced potatoes.

Turn up the heat and stir-fry the potatoes for 5 minutes. Add the salt, pepper and lemon juice and continue cooking for a further 5 minutes, stirring constantly.

Waxy potatoes. Serves 6. Vegetarian dish.

In this unusual recipe the potatoes are first boiled and allowed to cool then diced and fried with the spices.

Potatoes with garlic and sesame *India*

900g (2 lb) small new potatoes
5 tbsp vegetable oil
1 tbsp sesame seeds
2 large cloves of garlic,
   peeled and chopped
½ tsp ground turmeric
1 tsp salt
Pinch of cayenne pepper

Wash the potatoes thoroughly but do not scrape. Cut them in half, rinse in cold water then dry. Heat the oil in a heavy frying pan over a medium heat and, when hot, put in the potatoes and cook for 10 minutes, stirring occasionally until lightly browned. Remove potatoes and keep warm.

Put the sesame seeds into the pan and stir, add the garlic and when it is starting to turn brown, add the turmeric, potatoes, salt and cayenne pepper. Stir well, cover and cook gently until the potatoes are tender.

New potatoes. Serves 6. Vegetarian dish.

This is a deliciously spicy way of using up all those tiny new potatoes, without having to scrape them!

Herbed potatoes *Belgium*

225g (8 oz) potatoes, hot and
   mashed
1 tsp thyme, finely chopped
1 tsp mint, finely chopped
1 tsp parsley, finely chopped
1 tsp marjoram, finely
   chopped
1 tsp basil, finely chopped
75g (3oz) Parmesan cheese,
   grated
1 tbsp fresh breadcrumbs
25g (1oz) butter

Put the hot, mashed potato through a mouli and mix together with the finely chopped herbs. Stir in the Parmesan, or any other strong cheese.

Place in a suitable dish, sprinkle the breadcrumbs over the mixture and dot with butter. Brown under a hot grill.

Floury potatoes. Serves 2. Vegetarian dish.

The quantities given for this recipe can be varied according to what herbs are available.

Hasselback potatoes

Sweden

(see above)

8 potatoes, about tablespoon
    size

110g (4oz) butter, melted

1 tsp salt

Good grinding of black
    pepper

1 tbsp mixed herbs, chopped

Heat the oven to Gas mark 6, 400°F (205°C). Peel the potatoes and place in cold water to prevent them from going brown. Take out and prepare one potato at a time, drying thoroughly. Place in a tablespoon and using a sharp knife slice the potato across its width in thin slices to within 1cm (½in) from the bottom; the spoon should help prevent you from slicing the potato all the way through.

Arrange the potatoes, cut side up, in a roasting tin, brush with half of the melted butter, season and bake for about 35 minutes until tender. Brush with the remaining melted butter and sprinkle the herbs over the top. Return to the oven and cook for a further 15 minutes, until nicely browned.

Floury potatoes. Serves 8. Vegetarian dish.

These unusual scored potatoes can be cooked round any joint of roast meat.

Caramelized potatoes　　　　*Denmark*

700g (1½ lb) potatoes
½ tsp salt
50g (2oz) sugar
75g (3oz) butter

Peel the potatoes and place in a large saucepan with water and salt. Bring to the boil then simmer gently for 15 minutes, until the potatoes are just cooked. Drain and dry off a little.

In a large frying pan, heat the sugar until lightly browned, or caramelized, stirring constantly. Add the butter and stir round the pan until melted. Add the potatoes and cook for about 10 minutes, shaking the pan carefully until all the potatoes are evenly coated.

Waxy or new potatoes. Serves 8. Vegetarian dish.

Serve these as a vegetable to accompany roast pork or beef.

Château potatoes (Pommes de terre château)　　*France*
(see page 49 for illustration)

700g (1½ lb) potatoes
175g (6oz) butter
Salt and pepper to taste
1 tbsp parsley, chopped

Select potatoes of a large, even size and peel them. Dry with a clean tea cloth. Melt the butter in a deep frying pan, add the potatoes, salt and pepper. Shake the pan to ensure the potatoes are coated with the butter.

Transfer to a casserole dish and bake in the oven Gas mark 4, 350°F (180°C), until golden brown.

Waxy, new or floury potatoes. Serves 6. Vegetarian dish.

Potato à la maitre d'hotel　　　*France*
(Pommes de terre à la maitre d'hotel)

450g (1 lb) potatoes
600ml (1 pt) milk
Salt and pepper to taste
110g (4oz) butter, in small
　　pieces
Parsley, chopped for garnish

Boil the potatoes in salted water. When cooked, drain then slice into a deep frying pan. Bring the milk to the boil and pour over the potatoes.

Season to taste. Dot the pieces of butter all over the top and cook at a simmer until the liquid has been boiled off and absorbed. Pile into a warm serving dish and garnish with parsley.

Waxy or new potatoes. Serves 4. Vegetarian dish.

Potatoes à la paysanne　　　*France*
(Pommes de terre à la paysanne)

450g (1 lb) potatoes
110g (4oz) sorrel, chopped
25g (1oz) chervil, chopped
1 clove of garlic, crushed
50g (2oz) butter
Salt and pepper to taste
25g (1oz) butter for topping
600ml (1 pt) beef stock

Peel the potatoes and cut into very thin slices. Gently sauté the sorrel, chervil and garlic in the 50g (2oz) of butter until softened.

Layer the potato slices with the herbs in a casserole dish. Season with salt and pepper. Pour over the beef stock. Flake the 25g (1oz) butter over the top, cover, and bake in the oven Gas mark 4, 350°F (180°C) for 1 hour.

Waxy or floury potatoes. Serves 4. Substitute the beef stock for a vegetarian dish.

Crunchy roast potatoes · *Scotland*

(see below)

450g (1 lb) potatoes, peeled
Hot dripping to roast*
110g (4oz) fresh white
   breadcrumbs, sieved
1 tbsp mixed herbs, chopped

Cut the potatoes into even pieces and parboil in salted water for 8 minutes. Drain and allow to dry off.

Heat the dripping, or any other suitable fat, in a deep roasting tin. Put the potatoes into the dripping and roast in the oven Gas mark 5, 375°F (190°C) for 30 minutes basting occasionally with the hot fat. Mix together the sieved breadcrumbs and mixed herbs. Carefully remove the part-cooked potatoes from the fat and roll them in the breadcrumb mixture. Return to the roasting tin and continue to cook until nicely browned.

Floury or waxy potatoes. Serves 4. *Substitute the dripping for a vegetarian dish.

Rosti · *Switzerland*

450g (1 lb) potatoes, boiled
Pork lard, or oil
Finely diced onion may be added to this dish, if required.

Pass the cooked potatoes through a ricer or sieve. Heat the lard or oil in a heavy frying pan. Flatten the potatoes into a cake shape in the pan and cook until well-browned on the underside.

Carefully turn upside down so that the brown side is uppermost, on to a plate.

Floury potatoes. Serves 4. Substitute vegetable oil for a vegetarian dish.

Potatoes Lorette (Pommes de terre Lorette) · *France*

1 batch Dauphine potato
   mixture, see page 63
Fat for deep frying

Shape the Dauphin potato mixture into small crescent shapes, each weighing about 50g (2oz) and fry in hot fat until nicely browned. Drain on absorbent paper.

Floury potatoes. Serves 8.

Duchess potatoes (Pommes de terre Duchesse) *France*

(see page 49 for illustration)

450g (1 lb) potatoes, peeled
50g (2oz) butter
Salt and pepper to taste
1 medium egg and 2 medium egg yolks, beaten
½ tsp nutmeg, grated

Boil the potatoes in salted water until cooked. Drain, dry on a clean tea cloth and rub through a sieve. Add the butter, salt, pepper, beaten egg and yolks and nutmeg. Mix thoroughly with a wooden spoon. When required, brush with beaten egg and brown lightly in the oven Gas mark 4, 350°F (180°C).

Floury potatoes. Serves 4.

This mixture can be piped through a forcing bag, or moulded by hand, and brushed with a little beaten egg before browning in the oven. It can also be used to form borders round the edge of a serving dish, and freezes well.

Potato borders (Bordures de pommes de terre) *France*

1 batch Duchess potato mixture, see above
1 medium egg, beaten

Put the potato into a forcing bag fitted with a star nozzle and pipe round the borders of a serving dish. Brush with beaten egg and brown lightly in the oven Gas mark 4, 350°F (180°C).

Croquette potatoes *France*

(see below)

900g (2 lb) Duchess mixture, see above
25g (1oz) plain flour
1 medium egg, beaten with 70ml (2½ fl oz) milk
110g (4oz) breadcrumbs
Watercress to garnish

Divide the Duchess potato mixture into 25g (1oz) pieces and roll into a cork shape.

Roll in the flour, then the egg and milk and finally in the breadcrumbs.

Place in a chip basket and deep fry in hot fat until golden brown. Drain and garnish with the watercress.

Floury potatoes. Serves 6.

Potato balls

350g (12oz) potatoes, cooked
and mashed
5 tsp Parmesan cheese or
Geska
2 tsp mild curry powder
1 tsp mixed herbs
3 tbsp onion, finely chopped
Fresh wholemeal
breadcrumbs

Thoroughly mix together all the ingredients, except the bread-crumbs. Shape the mixture into balls about the size of a golf ball and coat with the breadcrumbs

Place on a well-greased tray and bake in the oven Gas mark 5, 375°F (190°C) for 40 minutes. Allow to cool for 10 minutes before serving.

Floury potatoes. Makes 8. Vegetarian dish.

If you wish to use these savoury balls cold with a salad, roll in poppy or sesame seeds instead of breadcrumbs before baking. Chill well and serve with mayonnaise.

Cheesy potato balls

England

700g (1½ lb) potatoes, cooked
75g (3oz) butter
110g (4 oz) cheese, grated
1 tsp salt
Good grinding of black
pepper
5 medium eggs, hard-boiled
1 tbsp parsley or chervil,
chopped
1 tbsp chives, chopped
1 medium egg, beaten
Fresh brown breadcrumbs
Vegetable oil

Mash the hot, cooked potato with the butter, cheese, salt and pepper. Grate the hard-boiled eggs on a coarse grater and blend into the potato mixture. Add the herbs, divide the mixture into ten small pieces and roll into balls.

Roll in the beaten egg and coat with breadcrumbs. Heat the oil in a frying pan and cook the balls until golden brown. Serve with a green salad.

Floury potatoes. Makes 10.

Turkish potato balls

Turkey

450g (1 lb) potatoes, peeled
1 medium egg, plus 1 yolk
110g (4 oz) cottage cheese
1 tbsp parsley, chopped
1 tsp salt
Good grinding of black
pepper
50g (2oz) fresh breadcrumbs
Oil for frying
Parsley sprigs for garnish

Peel the potatoes, cook until tender then put through a ricer or mouli. Mix in the whole egg, cottage cheese, parsley and seasoning.

Take small pieces of the mixture and shape to the size of a golf ball, roll in the egg yolk, then in the breadcrumbs and fry in the hot oil until golden brown. Fry the sprigs of parsley in the hot oil for 1 minute until crisp and use as a garnish.

Floury potatoes. Serves 4.

Byron potatoes (Pommes de terre Byron)   *France*
(see above)

6 large potatoes, scrubbed

Salt and good grinding of black pepper

1 tbsp olive oil

75g (3oz) butter

110g (4oz) Parmesan cheese, grated

150ml (5fl oz) double cream

Boil the potatoes in their jackets until just tender. Peel and roughly break up with a fork and season with salt and pepper.

Mould into round cakes. Heat the oil and butter in a deep frying pan. When the fat froths, add the potatoes cakes and cook until golden brown. Put them into a casserole dish and sprinkle over the cheese.

Bake in the oven Gas mark 7, 425°F (220°C), for about 15 minutes until nicely browned and glazed on the top.

Floury potatoes. Serves 6. Vegetarian dish.

Potatoes à la landaise   *France*
(Pommes de terre à la landaise)

75g (3oz) goose fat, chicken fat or lard

175g (6oz) onions, diced

175g (6oz) Bayonne ham, diced

700g (1½ lb) potatoes, cooked and cut into large dice

2 large cloves garlic, crushed

Salt and pepper to taste

1 tbsp parsley, chopped

Heat the fat in a deep pan and fry the onions and ham until nicely browned. Stir in the diced potatoes, garlic, salt and pepper. Cover with a lid and cook slowly for about 30 minutes, stirring from time to time. Turn into a serving dish and garnish with the chopped parsley.

Waxy potatoes. Serves 6.

Potato quenelles with Parmesan

(Quenelles de pommes de terre au Parmesan)

France

2 medium eggs
500g (1 lb 2oz) potatoes,
   cooked and sieved
75g (3oz) flour
Salt and pepper to taste
1 tsp nutmeg, grated
Boiling, salted water
110g (4oz) butter, browned
50g (2oz) white breadcrumbs
50g (2oz) butter, melted
75g (3oz) Parmesan cheese,
   grated

To make the potato quenelles, beat the eggs thoroughly and stir into the sieved potatoes. Add the flour to make a firm paste. Season with salt, pepper and nutmeg.

Shape into small logs about 2.5cm (1in) in length and drop, one-by-one, into the boiling salted water. Poach for 10 minutes. Drain and set aside. Brown the butter but do not burn, add the breadcrumbs and cook lightly.

Butter a suitable serving dish and sprinkle with half the Parmesan cheese. Place the quenelles in the dish and pour over the butter and breadcrumbs mixture. Sprinkle the remainder of the Parmesan over the potatoes and pour the melted butter over. Place in the oven Gas mark 7, 425°F (220°C), until nicely browned.

Floury potatoes. Serves 6.

Milanese croquettes (Croquettes milanaises)

France

6 medium potatoes, scrubbed
50g (2oz) butter
25g (1oz) flour
255ml (10fl oz) hot milk
3 medium eggs, separated
110g (4oz) cooked lean ham,
   cut into pieces
110g (4oz) cheese, grated
Salt and pepper to taste
Toasted breadcrumbs to coat
Oil for deep frying
1 tbsp parsley, chopped

Boil the potatoes in their skins until just tender. Melt the butter in a deep pan, add the flour and stir to a paste over the heat, then cook for 2 minutes. Remove from the heat and gradually add the hot milk. Return to the heat and bring to the boil, cooking until the sauce has thickened. Remove from the heat, add the egg yolks, ham, cheese, salt and pepper.

Put the potatoes through a sieve or mouli, then beat into the sauce and leave until quite cold. Shape the mixture into egg-sized balls. Whip the egg white lightly, roll the croquettes in the egg white, then the toasted breacrumbs. Heat the oil until a blue haze can be seen then carefully drop the croquettes into the oil and cook until golden brown. Remove and drain on absorbent paper. Keep hot until all have been cooked. Garnish with parsley and serve immediately.

Floury potatoes. Serves 6.

Potatoes à l' hongroise

(Pommes de terre à l'hongroise)

France

110g (4oz) onions, chopped
50g (2oz) butter
1 large tomato, peeled, deseeded and chopped
1 level tsp paprika
700g (1½ lb) potatoes, peeled
   and thickly sliced
Salt and pepper to taste
600ml (1 pt) beef stock
2 tbsp parsley, chopped

Gently fry the onions in the butter until transparent. Add the chopped tomato and paprika and stir well. Stir in the potato slices, salt and pepper and pour the stock over the mixture.

Bake in the oven Gas mark 4, 350°F (180°C), for 1 hour until tender. Serve garnished with the chopped parsley.

Waxy potatoes. Serves 6. Substitute vegetable stock for a vegetarian dish.

Lyonnaise potatoes (Pommes de terre Lyonnaise) *France*
(see above)

900g (2 lb) potatoes
2 medium onions
4 tbsp olive oil
Salt and freshly ground black
   pepper
1 tbsp parsley, chopped

Boil the potatoes in their skins for 15 minutes. Peel and cut into even slices. Peel the onions and cut into thin rings.

Heat the oil in a deep frying pan and fry the onions until nicely browned. Remove from the pan with a draining spoon and keep warm. Add the potatoes to the pan and sprinkle with salt. Cook on both sides until golden brown, then add the onions. Season with a little more salt and a good grinding of black pepper. Turn into a serving dish. Garnish with chopped parsley.

Waxy potatoes. Serves 6. Vegetarian dish.

Potato and onion medley   *Australia*

18 small new potatoes,
   washed not scraped
18 pickling onions, peeled
2 tbsp chives, finely chopped
1 small carton natural yogurt
1 tbsp lemon juice
Salt and pepper to taste

Steam the potatoes and onions in a steaming basket for about 20 minutes, until cooked.

Combine the chives, yogurt, lemon juice, salt and pepper. When the potatoes and onions are ready, carefully coat with the dressing and serve very hot.

New potatoes. Serves 6. Vegetarian dish.

Crainquebille potatoes

France

(Pommes de terre Crainquebille)

450g (1 lb) onions, chopped
110g (4oz) butter
700g (1½ lb) potatoes, cut into long shapes
600ml (1 pt) white vegetable stock
Salt and pepper to taste
Bouquet garni
1 clove of garlic, crushed
4 tomatoes, sliced
110g (4oz) white breadcrumbs

Sauté the chopped onion in the butter until transparent but not browned. Slice the potatoes lengthwise and arrange over the onions. Pour the stock over, to come about halfway up the potatoes. Season with salt and pepper, add the bouquet garni and crushed garlic. Top each potato piece with a slice of deseeded tomato.

Bring to a gentle simmer, cover and cook for about 15 minutes until tender. Remove the lid and sprinkle the breadcrumbs over the top of the mixture. Brown under a hot grill.

Waxy potatoes. Serves 6. Vegetarian dish.

Champ

Ireland

5 large potatoes, peeled
1 large onion
350ml (12fl oz) buttermilk, or milk
6 medium spring onions, finely sliced
110g (4oz) butter
1 tsp salt
Good grinding of black pepper

Cook the potatoes in salted water until just tender. Drain, allow to dry off then mash them.

Finely grate the onion and cook in the milk for 3 to 4 minutes. Add the milk and onion to the potato and beat to a creamy consistency. Stir in the spring onions, butter and season to taste.

Floury potatoes. Serves 6. Vegetarian dish.

This recipe calls for the use of buttermilk, but whole milk can be used if this is not readily available.

Creamy fried potatoes

Sweden

4 large potatoes
1 large onion
50g (2oz) butter
275ml (10fl oz) water
150ml (5fl oz) double cream
1 tsp salt
Good grinding of black pepper
2 tbsp fresh parsley, chopped

Peel and cut the potatoes into about 1cm (½in) cubes. Finely chop the onion. Melt the butter in a large frying pan over a fairly high heat and sauté the potatoes and onion, shaking the pan from time to time until the potatoes are a light golden brown. Add half of the water and cook uncovered for about 10 minutes, or until the water has evaporated. If the potatoes are not sufficiently cooked, add the other half of the water and again allow it to evaporate.

Pour the cream over the potato and onion mixture, season with salt and pepper and bring almost, but not quite, to the boil. Simmer gently for a further 5 minutes, until the cream has thickened into a smooth sauce. Spoon into a serving dish and garnish with the parsley.

Waxy potatoes. Serves 6. Vegetarian dish.

Potato purée (Aligot) *France*

(see below)

700g (1½ lb) potatoes, peeled weight
75g (3oz) butter
175g (6oz) Cantal cheese, thinly sliced
1 clove of garlic, crushed
Salt and freshly ground black pepper
2 tbsp double cream

Cook the potatoes in their skins until tender. Peel and sieve. Return to the pan. Over a medium heat add the butter, in small pieces, mixing well and increasing the heat until very hot.

When all the butter has been melted and mixed with the potatoes, take the pan off the heat and add the thin slices of cheese, the crushed garlic and salt and pepper to taste.

Continue stirring and lifting up the mixture, so that the cheese is pulled into the purée, putting the pan back on to the heat occasionally to keep the contents hot. Add the cream, working and pulling the purée up in the air for about 10 minutes. Serve very hot to accompany grilled meats of any kind.

Floury potatoes. Serves 6. Vegetarian dish.

I think the most renowned French potato dish is Aligot which comes from the Auvergne region of France. The French housewife is praised for her housekeeping and sound economical habits. Aligot was traditionally eaten on a Friday when it replaced both meat and fish.

Dauphin potatoes (Pommes de terre Dauphines) *France*

175g (6oz) choux pastry, see page 140
450g (1 lb) Duchess potato mix, see page 57
75g (3oz) plain flour
1 medium egg, beaten
175g (6oz) fresh breadcrumbs
Oil for frying

Beat together the choux pastry and cold Duchess potato mixture. Shape into small balls. Coat with flour, dip in beaten egg, roll in breadcrumbs and fry until golden brown.

Floury potatoes. Serves 8.

Main meals and supper dishes

Although I have called this section of the book 'main meals and supper dishes', I must stress that, as stated earlier, the potato makes more expensive ingredients go a long way. It therefore follows that the recipes for main dishes can be reduced to make supper dishes and supper dishes can be stretched to make main meals. The potato is particularly useful for this purpose, as it is available all the year round and I would say that it must be classed as the original convenience food. Try adapting some of the recipes to include your own choice of ingredients as, in many cases, the precise quantities are not too important. Be imaginative and enjoy your own creativity.

From the wide selection of meals given in this section, I would recommend that you try the asparagus and potato quiche on page 74. It is an ideal main course, supper dish or picnic food. This is also true of the spinach flan on page 76. The casserole dishes, of course, are made mainly with the addition of potatoes, which means they do not need to be cooked separately, thus saving on fuel.

The recipes using potatoes as a topping, where mashed potatoes are creamed and perhaps leeks, swedes or parsnips mixed in with them, are a great way of making a complete course. This type of dish will freeze well for up to three months. I usually make my fish pies to store in this way as well as other pies with potato topping. Croquettes, with the addition of some left-over vegetables, will also freeze well and are very convenient to use in an emergency.

The potato and beetroot pie from Russia, on page 72, was a delightful surprise to me and my family! I also served it as an extra 'filling' dish for a group of my son's friends and I was asked several times if there was any more. I have always adored hot, buttered beetroot as a vegetable and as we grow beetroot in the garden, and usually have plenty of it, it is nice to find another popular family recipe for its use, other than pickling in vinegar.

Opposite: see page 85 for
Potato and pepper scramble recipe.

Bubble and squeak *England*

1 small cabbage
450g (1 lb) cooked potatoes
25g (1oz) butter
Salt and pepper to taste
Leftover vegetables, if
  available, cooked
Bacon fat or beef dripping
  for frying

Cut, core and finely shred the cabbage. Wash it well then plunge into boiling water and cook for about 5 minutes. Drain thoroughly in a collander.

Mash the potatoes, butter, salt and pepper. When smooth add the cabbage together with any leftover vegetables and mix well. Using a potato scoop as a measure, divide the mixture into about 6 portions. Place in hot fat and flatten. Fry for about 5 minutes, turn over and fry the other side for about 5 minutes. Serve piping hot.

Floury potatoes. Serves 2. Substitute the fat for a vegetarian dish.

A favourite dish which, during the depression of the 30s, was made from leftover vegetables and served as a main meal. The name comes from the squeaky noise made by the cabbage as it is fried. Traditionally served on washday Mondays!

Colcannon *Ireland*

225g (8 oz) potatoes, peeled
  and cubed
225g (8 oz) swedes, peeled
  and cubed
225g (8 oz) carrots, peeled
  and cubed
110g (4 oz) cabbage, shredded
50g (2oz) butter
1 tbsp spicy brown table sauce

Cook all the vegetables together until tender. Drain well and mash thoroughly, adding the butter and brown sauce. Serve piping hot.

Floury potatoes. Serves 4. Vegetarian dish.

Vegetables have long been the mainstay of the Irish and this recipe is both inexpensive and tasty. Serve as an accompaniment to hot or cold meats, or on its own as a simple supper dish.

Clapshot *Scotland*

450g (1 lb) potatoes
450g (1 lb) swedes
Salt and pepper to taste
50g (2oz) dripping
1 tbsp chives, chopped

Cook the potatoes and swedes together until tender. Drain well and mash. Add the seasoning and beat in the dripping. Stir in the chopped chives and serve piping hot.

Floury potatoes. Serves 4. Substitute the dripping for a vegetarian dish.

This is the traditional accompaniment to haggis, although it is more often called 'bashed tatties and neeps'.

Kailkenny *Scotland*

225g (8 oz) potatoes, boiled
225g (8 oz) kale or cabbage,
  cooked
110ml (4fl oz) double cream
Salt and pepper to taste

Mash the potatoes thoroughly and mix in the cooked kale, or cabbage, which has been finely chopped after cooking. Stir in the double cream, season with salt and pepper. Serve very hot.

Floury potatoes. Serves 2. Vegetarian dish.

The vegetable commonly known as 'kale' is referred to as 'kail' in Scotland, hence the difference in the spelling of the title and the ingredients.

66

Potatoes with cauliflower and eggs   *Iran*

450g (1 lb) cauliflower

115g (4oz) creamed coconut block, grated

275ml (10fl oz) warm water

2.5cm (1in) cube of fresh ginger, peeled and chopped

4 cloves of garlic, crushed

55ml (2fl oz) water

4 tbsp vegetable oil

1 level tsp ground cinnamon

1 medium onion, peeled and diced

2 small green chillies, deseeded and chopped

2 medium tomatoes, peeled and diced

1 level tsp ground turmeric

4 medium potatoes, peeled and par-boiled, cooled

Juice of a fresh lemon

1 tsp garam masala, see page 26

1 tsp salt

6 medium eggs, hard-boiled

Divide the cauliflower into florets and cook in boiling salted water for 1 minute, strain and cool under cold running water. Dissolve the grated coconut cream in the warm water. Using a food processor if available, make a paste with the ginger, garlic and 55ml (2fl oz) of water.

Heat the oil in a large frying pan and fry the cinnamon, onion, ginger and garlic paste and chopped chillies for 2 minutes. Add the tomatoes, turmeric and coconut milk. Cover the pan and let the mixture cook slowly for 15 minutes.

Add the potatoes cut into quarters lengthways, cauliflower, lemon juice, garam masala and salt. Stir carefully and cook for a further 5 minutes. Cut the hard-boiled eggs in half and place cut side up in the mixture, and spoon over some of the sauce. Serve with crusty bread.

Waxy potatoes. Serves 6.

Potato and vegetables with chilli sauce   *Sumatra*

2 tsp chilli powder

2 medium onions, finely chopped

3 cloves of garlic, crushed

2 tsp Laos powder

2 tbsp groundnut oil

2 tomatoes, skinned, deseeded and chopped

Pinch sea salt

425ml (15fl oz) thick coconut milk – made with creamed coconut block mixed with 330ml (12fl oz) of water, until dissolved

3 curry leaves

175g (6oz) green cabbage, shredded

175g (6oz) French beans, sliced

175g (6oz) potatoes, peeled and cubed

Substitute ½tsp ground ginger and large pinch black pepper for Laos powder, if unavailable.

Put the chilli powder, onion, garlic, Laos powder, or substitute, and oil in a blender, or food processor, and blend to a smooth paste. Fry the paste in a wok or large frying pan, stirring continually, until lightly browned. Add the tomatoes and stir. Season to taste. Pour in coconut milk, made with creamed coconut block mixed with 330ml (12fl oz) of water until dissolved. Add the curry leaves and bring slowly to the boil.

Add the vegetables and simmer uncovered, for about 20 minutes, until the potatoes are just tender.

Waxy potatoes. Serves 4. Vegetarian dish.

Stir-fried potatoes with broccoli *India*

(see below)

900g (2 lb) potatoes, peeled
and cooked

450g (1 lb) fresh or frozen
broccoli, in sprigs

110g (4oz) green beans, sliced

6 tbsp vegetable oil

½ tsp whole black mustard
seeds

110g (4oz) sweetcorn

50g (2oz) celery, chopped

110g (4oz) red pepper,
chopped

1 large onion, peeled and
chopped

2 cloves garlic, peeled and
crushed

1 tsp garam masala, see page
26

Small pinch cayenne pepper

Pinch of salt

Allow the potatoes to cool. Cook the broccoli and green beans until just tender then freshen under cold running water and drain.

Heat the oil in a large non-stick frying pan, or wok, and when very hot throw in the mustard seeds. When they begin to 'pop', add the broccoli, green beans, sweetcorn, celery, red pepper, onion and garlic. Turn down the heat and stir fry for about 10 minutes. Season with the garam masala, cayenne pepper and salt. Continue stirring and frying until thoroughly heated.

Waxy or new potatoes. Serves 6. Vegetarian dish.

I have used broccoli in this recipe because we grow so much in the garden but almost any green vegetable could be substituted.
It is traditional in the North of India to cook potatoes and greens together. Try fenugreek greens as these are perhaps more authentic.

Paprika potatoes

Hungary

450g (1 lb) potatoes, peeled and thinly sliced
2 tbsp cooking oil
450g (1 lb) leeks, washed and thinly sliced
275g (10oz) mushrooms, quartered
½ tsp paprika
Salt and pepper to taste
150ml (5fl oz) soured cream to garnish

Cook the potatoes in salted, boiling water for 10 minutes. Drain off and keep the liquid.

Warm the oil and gently fry the leeks, mushrooms and paprika for 8 minutes, stirring frequently. To this mixture add the sliced potatoes and combine carefully. Continue to cook for a further 5 minutes, adding a little of the potato liquor, as necessary. Season to taste but remember that the liquor has already been salted. Serve piping hot with the soured cream swirled all over the top.

Waxy potatoes. Serves 4. Vegetarian dish.

This warming dish uses paprika, which is obtained from grinding sweet red peppers. It can be used liberally as, unlike some other red peppers it is not very hot. Hungarians use this spice in their world famous dish, 'gulyas' or 'goulash'. This vegetarian version is delicious and should be accompanied by a crisp, green salad.

Potato and breadcrumb omelette

Spain

6 medium potatoes
50g (2oz) butter
Yolks of 6 medium eggs
Whites of 4 medium eggs
50g (2oz) fresh breadcrumbs
Salt and pepper to taste

Boil the potatoes until tender, then drain and dry off. Mash well with 25g (1oz) of the butter. Add breadcrumbs, yolks and whites of eggs, seasoning and mix well with the potato.

Melt remaining butter in an omelette pan and pour in the potato mixture and cook for 5 minutes, stirring gently, until almost set. Finish by placing under a very hot grill until nicely browned.

Floury potatoes. Serves 4.

Kookoo with potatoes and herbs

Iran

3 medium potatoes
1 tsp salt
Good grinding of black pepper
3 tbsp vegetable oil
8 medium eggs
½ tsp bicarbonate of soda
2 tbsp fresh parsley, chopped
1 tbsp fresh chives, chopped
3 spring onions, finely sliced white and a little green

Peel and, using a mandolin, finely slice the potatoes. Line the bottom of a nonstick frying pan with overlapping slices of the potato, going round in circles and overlapping each circle. Season with salt and pepper and dribble the oil over the potatoes. Cover, and over a low heat cook the potatoes for about 10 minutes.

In the meantime, beat the eggs well, add the bicarbonate of soda, parsley, chives, spring onions and the rest of the salt and pepper. Pour the egg mixture over the potatoes, cover the pan and continue to cook over a fairly low heat for a further 25 minutes, or until the egg mixture is well set. Carefully slide the kookoo on to a serving plate and cut into wedges. Serve hot or cold.

Waxy potatoes. Serves 6.

Kookoo is an Iranian version of an omelette, although it is perhaps closer to a soufflé. Cut into wedges it makes an excellent picnic food.

Potato cake sandwich
(see above)

Australia

225g (8 oz) potatoes, cooked and sieved

1 medium egg, beaten

Salt and pepper to taste

Oil for frying

2 rashers grilled bacon

2 lightly fried eggs

Mix the sieved potatoes with the beaten egg and season. Divide into four equal portions and form into patties or cakes. Cover with cling film and leave in the refrigerator for at least 2 hours, then fry in hot fat until nicely golden and heated all through.

Sandwich the grilled bacon and eggs between the cakes.

Floury potatoes. Serves 2.

Spiced potato rissoles *India*

225g (8 oz) potatoes
1 medium egg, beaten
1½ tsp salt
1 tsp garam masala, see
    page 26
2 tsp parsley, chopped
½ tsp chilli powder
Oil for shallow frying

4 spring onions, finely
    chopped
1 tbsp lemon juice
175g (6oz) fresh or defrosted
    peas, slightly mashed
1 tsp ground ginger

Spiced potato pastry: cook the potatoes in their skins until just tender. When cool enough to handle, peel then rub through a sieve or mouli, or just mash very thoroughly. Beat the egg into the potatoes until the mixture resembles a smooth pastry. Mix together the salt, garam masala, chopped parsley and chilli powder. Sprinkle the herb mixture over the pastry and knead once more to combine all the ingredients. Set aside for 2 hours.

Rissoles: add the remaining ingredients to the pastry mix. Shape into small rissole shapes and fry in medium hot oil until golden brown in colour. Drain and serve hot or cold.

Floury potatoes. Makes 8.

Potato kephtides *Greece*

450g (1 lb) cold potatoes,
    mashed
25g (1oz) butter, melted
3 spring onions, chopped
2 large tomatoes, peeled,
    deseeded and diced
50g (2oz) flour
Salt and pepper to taste
Olive oil for frying

Pass the mashed potato through a sieve. Add all the other ingredients to the potato and mix well.

Heat the oil. Divide the mixture into 8 portions and shape into small, flat cakes. Fry until golden brown. Drain and serve hot.

Floury potatoes. Makes 8. Vegetarian dish.

Potato Scotch eggs *England*

500g (1¼ lb) duchess potato
    mixture, see page 57
4 medium eggs, hard-boiled
1 medium egg, beaten
Fresh brown breadcrumbs
Few chopped chives
Vegetable oil

Divide the potato mixture into four and make a parcel round each hard-boiled egg. Coat with beaten egg, then roll in the breadcrumbs and chives mixed together.

Heat the oil in a deep frying pan and cook each egg for about 5 minutes. Drain well on absorbent paper.

Floury potatoes. Serves 4.

Cheese and potato soufflé *England*

700g (1½ lb) potatoes, boiled
150g (5oz) cheese, grated
3 medium eggs, separated
25g (1oz) butter, softened
2 tbsp milk
1 tsp ready-made English
    mustard
Pinch of salt
1 level tsp cayenne pepper

Put the cooked potatoes through a vegetable mouli or ricer. Beat in the cheese, egg yolks, butter, milk and mustard. Whisk the egg whites until stiff and carefully fold into the potato mixture; season with salt and cayenne pepper, then gently pour into a well-buttered soufflé dish.

Cook in the oven Gas mark 7, 425°F (220°C) for 40 minutes. Resist the temptation to open the oven door before the cooking time is up. Serve immediately.

Floury potatoes. Serves 4.

Potato cobbler   *Scotland*

(see opposite)

110g (4oz) butter, softened
225g (8oz) self raising flour, sifted
Pinch salt
225g (8oz) potato, cooked and sieved
1 medium egg, lightly beaten

Rub the butter into the sifted flour, add the salt and knead together with the potato to form a scone type dough. Roll out on a lightly floured board to about 1cm (½in) thick.

Cut into rounds and cover the casserole or pie-dish by making a lid of overlapping dough rounds. Brush over with the beaten egg and bake as required.

Floury potatoes. Serves 4.

I have named this unusual pie crust in remembrance of my first and only attempt to climb the famous Scottish mountain of that name – the Cobbler! This recipe can be used to make a savoury pie or, equally, a fruit or fish pie.

Potato and beetroot pie   *U.S.S.R.*

700g (1½ lb) potatoes, cooked and sliced
225g (8oz) beetroot, cooked and sliced
275ml (10fl oz) thick onion sauce, ready-made
50g (2oz) cheese, grated
Dried breadcrumbs

Fill a lightly buttered casserole dish with layers of potatoes and beetroot slices. Pour over the onion sauce. Cover the top with grated cheese and sprinkle with breadcrumbs.

Bake in the oven Gas mark 5, 375°F (190°C) for 30 minutes, until nicely browned.

Waxy or floury potatoes. Serves 6. Vegetarian dish.

Vegetable pie   *Ireland*

350g (12oz) small new potatoes
2 carrots
110g (4 oz) peas, shelled
4 spring onions
110g (4 oz) green beans
2 tomatoes
Few sprigs of cauliflower
Salt and pepper to taste
75ml (3fl oz) vegetable stock
175g (6oz) shortcrust potato pastry, see page 140

Prepare all the vegetables, slicing the potatoes, carrots, onions, beans and tomatoes. Place in a pie dish and season to taste. Pour over the stock.

Cover with the pastry and bake in the oven Gas mark 6, 400°F (200°C) for 20 minutes, then reduce oven to Gas mark 4, 350°F (180°C) and cook for a further 30 minutes, until vegetables are tender.

New potatoes. Serves 4. Vegetarian dish.

Vegetable and cheese pie   *Belgium*

450g (1 lb) mixed, diced vegetables
4 medium eggs, hard-boiled
275ml (10fl oz) cheese sauce, ready-made
450g (1 lb) potatoes, mashed
1 tbsp cheese, grated

Put the vegetables into a greased pie dish and arrange the quartered hard-boiled eggs on top. Pour over the sauce and cover all with the mashed potato.

Sprinkle the grated cheese over the potato and bake in the oven Gas mark 5, 375°F (190°C) for about 30 minutes, until nicely browned.

Floury potatoes. Serves 4.

Curried egg and potato pie
New Zealand

225g (8oz) shortcrust potato pastry, see page 140
4 medium eggs, hard-boiled
40g (1½oz) butter
40g (1½oz) plain flour
2 tsp curry powder
225ml (8fl oz) milk
2 tbsp sweetcorn
Salt and pepper to taste

Roll out half of the pastry and use it to line a 20cm (8in) flan tin or dish. Cut the eggs into slices and arrange overlapping in the pastry.

Make a sauce by melting the butter then blending in the flour and curry powder. Remove from the heat and carefully blend in the milk until smooth. Add the sweetcorn and season with salt and pepper. Return to the heat and, stirring occasionally, bring to the boil and allow to cook for about 2 minutes. Pour the curry sauce over the layered eggs and allow to cool. When only just warm, top with the rest of the pastry. Pinch the edges together to seal well and cut a small cross in the centre to allow the steam to escape.

Bake in the oven Gas mark 6, 400°F (200°C) for 20 minutes. Remove from the oven and brush top with a little cold milk. Return to the oven and bake for a further 15 minutes. Serve hot or cold.

Floury potatoes. Serves 6.

Czech potato pie (Bramborak)
Czechoslovakia

450g (1 lb) potatoes, peeled and grated
3 tbsp top of the milk
50g (2oz) flour
1 large clove of garlic, crushed
1 medium onion, peeled and grated
Salt and pepper to taste
50g (2oz) butter

Drain any excess liquid from the grated potatoes. Mix together the milk and flour and add the grated potatoes. Stir in the crushed garlic, onion and seasoning.

Place in a well-greased pie dish. Dot with butter and bake in the oven Gas mark 6, 400°F (200°C) for about 30 minutes until nicely browned on top. Alternatively, drop spoonfuls of the mixture into hot fat and fry on both sides.

Waxy potatoes. Serves 4. Vegetarian dish.

This makes a filling meal for a meatless day, or if you are on an economy drive! It was a favourite dish during the days of meat rationing.

Asparagus and potato quiche
England
(see opposite)

175g (6oz) short potato pastry, see page 140
3 medium eggs, beaten
1 large potato, peeled and grated
150ml (5fl oz) single cream
Salt and pepper to taste
450g (1 lb) tin of asparagus spears
Fresh parsley for garnish

Grease and line a 20cm (8in) quiche tin with the pastry. Bake blind in the oven Gas mark 4, 350°F (180°C) until golden brown and allow to cool slightly.

Mix together the beaten eggs, grated potato, cream, salt and pepper. Pour into the quiche tin and arrange the asparagus spears in a circle in the case, like the spokes of a wheel. Bake in the oven Gas mark 7, 425°F (220°C) for 10 minutes, reduce heat to Gas mark 4, 350°F (180°C) and bake for a further 30 minutes. Serve garnished with chopped parsley.

Floury potatoes. Serves 6.

This quiche has a delicate flavour and, served with a crisp green salad and crusty bread, makes a delicious midday meal but I must confess that I enjoy any leftovers cold for breakfast! You can substitute leeks for asparagus.

Spinach flan with potato pastry   *Italy*

175g (6oz) short potato pastry,
  see page 140
450g (1 lb) cooked and
  drained spinach *or* 225g
  (8oz) frozen spinach,
  defrosted, drained
3 medium eggs
150ml (5fl oz) double cream
Salt and pepper to taste
Parmesan cheese for garnish

Grease and line a 20cm (8in) flan dish with potato pastry and bake blind in the oven Gas mark 4, 350°F (180°C) until the pastry is a light golden colour. Remove from the oven and allow to cool.

In a liquidiser blend together the spinach, eggs, cream and seasoning. Pour into the cooled flan case, return to the oven at Gas mark 7, 425°F (220°C) for 7 minutes. Reduce heat to Gas mark 4, 350°F (180°C) and continue baking for a further 30 minutes until set. Sprinkle with Parmesan cheese.

Floury potatoes. Serves 6.

One of my friends cooked this flan for a school cheese and wine party. It proved so popular with everyone that she raised extra funds for the school by selling the recipe!

Mark's quick potato pizza   *England*
(see below)

110g (4 oz) potatoes, cooked
25g (1oz) butter
Pinch of salt
Good grinding of black
  pepper
110g (4 oz) self-raising flour
1 tbsp milk

Base: put the potatoes through a ricer or mouli then beat in the butter, salt and pepper until a creamy consistency is achieved. Slowly add the flour, then the milk, to form a fairly stiff dough. Roll out to about 20cm (8in) diameter and fry in a greased frying pan until the underside is slightly browned.

225g (8oz) tomatoes, skinned
  and sliced
1 onion, finely chopped
50g (2oz) mushrooms, sliced
110g (4 oz) strong cheese,
  grated
Few drops of olive oil

Filling: put the tomatoes on the potato base, then the onion and mushrooms. Scatter the cheese over. Carefully dribble a few drops of olive oil over the filling and place under a hot grill until the cheese has melted and browned.

Floury potatoes. Serves 6. Vegetarian dish.

Potato and cheese turnovers

Austria

225g (8 oz) oatmeal flour
Water, boiling and salted
3 medium potatoes, peeled
    and boiled
Salt to taste
225g (8 oz) cream cheese
1 tsp chives, chopped
275ml (10fl oz) milk
1 small onion
Cream or yogurt to serve

Put the flour into a basin and slowly add sufficient boiling, salted water to form a firm dough. Knead well for several minutes and with floured hands, shape into a large roll about 4cm (1½in) thick. Cut into pieces about 2.5cm (1in) in length and roll out flat. Sprinkle with a little flour and leave while you make the filling.

Rub the cooked potato through a sieve. Add the salt, cream cheese, chopped chives and milk. Finely chop the onion and add to the potato mixture. Combine all thoroughly. Place a spoonful of the potato on each flat piece of dough. Moisten the edges of the dough, then fold over and press the edges together to seal. Cook the turnovers in deep hot fat until golden. Serve hot with a side dish of cream or yogurt.

Floury potatoes. Serves 4. Vegetarian dish.

Austrians have a great deal of imagination and a love of good food. The variations they have discovered for using the humble potato seem to be infinite. I have only been able to include a few recipes in this book.

Potato Lorraine

England

450g (1 lb) potatoes, boiled
3 medium eggs
150ml (5fl oz) milk
Salt and pepper to taste
110g (4 oz) cheese, finely
    grated
1 tsp nutmeg, grated
150g (2oz) butter, softened
1 medium egg, hard-boiled
Anchovy fillets, optional

Slice the potatoes and line an ovenproof dish, making sure that the potatoes overlap. Beat the eggs, milk and seasoning and pour over the potatoes. Sprinkle over the grated cheese and nutmeg, and dot with small pieces of the softened butter.

Bake in the oven Gas mark 6, 400°F (200°C) until the custard sets. Remove from the oven and garnish with slices of hard-boiled egg and the anchovy fillets rolled into curls.

Waxy potatoes. Serves 4.

Lincolnshire stovies

England

800g (1¾ lb) potatoes
2 large onions
425ml (15fl oz) chicken stock
425ml (15fl oz) white sauce,
    ready-made
Salt and freshly ground
    pepper to taste
1 tsp fresh sage, chopped
50g (2oz) cheese, grated

Peel the potatoes and boil until almost cooked. Drain and allow to cool, then slice. Peel and slice the onions. Layer potato slices with a few slices of onion in a well-greased casserole dish. Continue layering until all the slices are used, finishing with a layer of potatoes.

Mix the chicken stock with the white sauce and pour over the potatoes and onions. Season well with salt and pepper and add the chopped sage. Sprinkle the top with grated cheese. Bake in the oven Gas mark 6, 400°F (200°C) and cook for 20 to 25 minutes, until the top is lightly browned.

Waxy potatoes. Serves 6. Substitute vegetable for chicken stock for a vegetarian dish.

Swiss potato and cheese savoury   *Switzerland*

450g (1 lb) potatoes, raw and
    grated
225g (8 oz) Swiss cheese,
    grated
1 tsp salt
Good grinding of black
    pepper
150ml (5fl oz) milk
½ tsp Tabasco sauce
1 tbsp parsley, chopped
1 tbsp chives, chopped

Mix together the grated potato and cheese and season with salt and pepper. Stir in the milk and Tabasco sauce and turn into a well-greased ovenproof dish.

Bake in the oven Gas mark 3, 325°F (170°C) for 1 hour, or until brown on top. To serve, turn upside down on to a plate and sprinkle with parsley and chives.

Floury potatoes. Serves 4. Vegetarian dish.

This beautiful country draws its culinary inspiration from a mixture of French, German and Italian cuisine, as served in holiday hotels and restaurants. Apart from catering to the tourist industry, the Swiss enjoy substantial meals and this recipe is just one using their delicious cheese.

Potato, cabbage and cheese bake   *Scotland*

450g (1 lb) potatoes, peeled
1 large onion, sliced
450g (1 lb) cabbage, shredded
75g (3oz) butter
1 tsp salt
Good grinding of pepper
75g (3oz) cheese, coarsely
    grated

Cook the potatoes and onion in a large pan of salted water. Strain and put aside but keep warm. Using the potato water, cook the cabbage until just tender. Drain thoroughly and reserve the water for making soup at a later date, if required.

Grease an ovenproof dish and layer the potatoes, onion and cabbage. dotting each layer with butter and salt and pepper to taste. Cover the top with grated cheese and bake in the oven Gas mark 5, 375°F (190°C) for 25 minutes.

Waxy or floury potatoes. Serves 4. Vegetarian dish.

Potato and spinach casserole   *Mexico*

Oil for greasing a dish
2 tbsp breadcrumbs, sieved
450g (1 lb) potatoes, cooked
    and mashed
3 tbsp cheese, grated
75g (3oz) butter
1 tsp salt
Good grinding of black
    pepper
1 medium egg yolk, beaten
450g (1 lb) fresh spinach
2 tsp cooking oil
1 small onion, finely chopped
1 tbsp tomato purée
1 green chilli, finely chopped
1 chicken stock cube
1 medium egg white, whisked
    until stiff
Pinch of nutmeg, grated

Grease an ovenproof dish and coat the inside surface all over with the breadcrumbs. Mix the mashed potato with the cheese, butter, salt, pepper and egg yolk and place in the casserole dish, over the breadcrumbs.

Wash and dry the spinach and remove any tough stalks. Chop up roughly. Heat the oil and fry the onion until soft but not browned. Add the spinach, tomato purée, chilli and crumbled stock cube and simmer gently for 5 minutes. Allow to cool until just warm, then fold in the whisked egg white and nutmeg. Pour the mixture over the potato and bake in the oven Gas mark 4, 350°F (180°C) for 25 minutes.

Floury potatoes. Serves 4.

This is a delicious recipe and despite the fact that spinach is not the most popular of vegetables, its nutritional value makes the dish worthy of inclusion. You may think the recipe is rather fiddly but I can assure you that the end result makes this justifiable.

Potato and turnip casserole   *Finland*

900g (2 lb) potatoes, peeled and sliced

900g (2 lb) turnips, peeled and sliced

600ml (1 pt) water

50g (2oz) self raising flour

75g (3oz) soft, white breadcrumbs

150ml (5fl oz) double cream

1 tbsp golden syrup

1 tbsp butter, melted

2 medium eggs, beaten

1 tsp salt

Good pinch of ground allspice, nutmeg and ginger

½ tsp white pepper

3 tbsp butter, melted

Put the potatoes, turnips and water into a large saucepan. Bring to the boil and cook over a low heat for about 25 minutes, until tender. Drain and retain the vegetable liquid. Thoroughly mash the potatoes and turnips until smooth, using an electric beater and adding about 150ml (5fl oz) of the vegetable liquid during the beating.

When smooth and creamy, gradually add all the other ingredients, including 1 tbsp melted butter. Place the mixture in a well-greased 2.4 lt (4 pt) casserole dish, level the top and drip the remaining 3 tbsp melted butter over the mixture. Bake in the oven without a lid Gas mark 2, 300°F (150°C) until the top is nicely browned.

Floury potatoes. Serves 8.

Cauliflower and potato dry curry   *Pakistan*

900g (2 lb) cauliflower

2 medium potatoes

2 tbsp oil for frying

10g (½oz) ginger, fresh or powdered

1 medium onion, chopped

1 tsp turmeric

2 tsp salt

½ tsp chilli powder

1 tsp garam masala, see page 26

Break the cauliflower into small florets, keeping a reasonable amount of stalk. Wash and drain. Peel the potatoes and cut into even-sized pieces.

Heat the oil in a deep drying pan and fry the onions and ginger. Add the turmeric and stir well. Add the cauliflower and potato pieces and cook for 10 minutes, stirring occasionally. Add the salt, chilli powder and garam masala, cover and cook for a further 10 minutes. Before serving drain off any surplus liquid.

Waxy or new potatoes. Serves 6. Vegetarian dish.

Vegetable curry with yogurt   *India*

225g (8oz) potatoes, peeled and diced

175g (6oz) carrots, peeled and sliced

175g (6oz) French beans, topped and tailed

175g (6oz) fresh or frozen green peas

4 green chillies, deseeded and chopped

275ml (10fl oz) water

Pinch of sea salt

Pinch of turmeric

Half a fresh coconut, grated

225ml (8fl oz) natural yogurt

Put all the vegetables, plus the salt and turmeric into a pan of boiling salted water, and bring to the boil. Cover and simmer until the vegetables are tender and most of the water has been absorbed. Mix the coconut and the yogurt together.

Remove the pan of vegetables from the heat and stir in the coconut and yogurt mixture. Bring the curry back to just below boiling point and serve immediately.

Waxy potatoes. Serves 4. Vegetarian dish.

Kipper cakes

(*see opposite*)

450g (1 lb) kippers
450g (1 lb) potatoes, mashed
2 medium eggs, hard-boiled
2 tbsp parsley, chopped
50g (2oz) butter, melted
Salt and freshly ground black
  pepper
1 medium egg, beaten
Breadcrumbs, fresh
Oil for frying

Gently steam the kippers between two plates over a pan of boiling water for 5 minutes. Carefully skin, bone and flake the fish and mix with the mashed potato.

Chop up the hard-boiled eggs, add to the fish and potato mixture together with the parsley, melted butter, salt and pepper. Shape into flat cakes, dip in the beaten egg, then in breadcrumbs and fry in a shallow pan with the oil until golden brown on each side.

Floury potatoes. Serves 6.

Cabbie claw

Scotland

450g (1 lb) fillet of cod
1 tsp horseradish root,
  grated
1 tbsp parsley, chopped
Salt and pepper to taste
25g (1oz) butter
450g (1 lb) hot potatoes,
  mashed
A little milk

25g (1oz) butter
25g (1oz) self raising flour
275ml (10fl oz) milk
1 medium egg, hard-boiled
Cayenne pepper

Fish mixture: put the fish in a saucepan with the horseradish, parsley, salt and pepper and sufficient water to cover. Bring to the boil, then simmer for about 15 minutes until the fish is cooked. Lift out the fish, retain the liquid, remove the skin and bones and flake roughly. Put on to a hot, shallow dish and keep warm. In the meantime, beat the butter into the mashed potato with sufficient milk to give a creamy consistency. Fork the potato mixture round the fish, or pipe a border, and keep warm.

Sauce: melt the butter, stir in the flour and gradually add the milk to 150ml (5fl oz) of the strained fish liquid. Bring to the boil and cook for 3 minutes. Chop the hard-boiled egg white and stir into the sauce with salt and pepper to taste. Gently pour the sauce over the fish. Sieve the egg yolk and sprinkle, together with the cayenne pepper, over the top of the sauce.

Floury potatoes. Serves 4.

This was a traditional supper dish often served to coachmen when arriving at great country houses.

Fish and potato eggs

Sweden

Deep fat or oil to fry
225g (8oz) cooked cod fillet
450g (1 lb) potatoes, mashed
A little milk to bind
Salt and pepper to taste
1 medium egg, beaten
Fresh dry breadcrumbs

Heat the fat or oil until just smoking. Skin, bone and flake the cod and mix with the mashed potato, adding a little milk to bind and seasoning to taste.

Divide the mixture into equal portions and form each into the shape of an egg. Coat with the beaten egg, then roll in breadcrumbs. Fry in the fat until nicely brown all over..

Floury potatoes. Serves 4.

Potato and cockle pie

England

1 large onion, chopped
25g (1oz) butter
50g (2oz) flour
425ml (15fl oz) milk
350g (12oz) cockles, fresh
1 tbsp parsley, finely chopped
1 tbsp chives, finely chopped
Salt and freshly ground black
    pepper
450g (1 lb) potatoes, cooked
4 tbsp cream or top of the
    milk
50g (2oz) cheese, grated
2 tbsp fresh breadcrumbs

Fry the onion in the butter until soft and transparent. Stir in the flour and remove from the heat. Slowly blend in the milk. Return to a medium heat and stir continuously until the sauce thickens, then allow to cook for 2 minutes. Add the well-rinsed cockles, parsley, chives and seasoning.

Put into an ovenproof dish. Mash the potatoes, mix well with the cream and spread over the cockles. Sprinkle the cheese and breadcrumbs on top of the potato and bake in the oven Gas mark 6, 400°F (200°C) for 20 minutes, until heated through and golden brown on top.

Floury potatoes. Serves 4.

Old English fish pie

England

450g (1 lb) smoked haddock
450g (1 lb) cod
40g (1½oz) butter
40g (1½oz) flour
275ml (10fl oz) milk
1 tsp anchovy essence
75g (3oz) cheese, grated
2 tbsp parsley, chopped
Salt and pepper to taste
700g (1½ lb) potatoes,
    mashed

Cook the fish with just enough water to cover for about 15 minutes. Drain the fish and save 275ml (10fl oz) of the fish stock. Skin, bone and flake the fish and place in an ovenproof casserole, which has been well buttered.

Make a sauce by melting the butter and stirring in the flour. Allow to cook for 1 minute, then stir in the milk and fish stock. Bring to the boil, stirring constantly, until thick and creamy. Continue cooking for 2 minutes. Add the anchovy essence, cheese, parsley and season to taste.

Pour the sauce over the fish and spread the mashed potato over the top of the dish. Roughly score the top with a fork and dot with butter. Bake in the oven Gas mark 4, 350°F (180°C) for 40 minutes, or until the top is golden brown.

Floury potatoes. Serves 6.

Cullen skink

Scotland

225g (8oz) potatoes, peeled
    and diced
1 large onion, peeled and
    diced
425ml (15fl oz) milk
450g (1 lb) smoked haddock
    fillet, skinned
Salt and pepper to taste
25g (1oz) butter

Put the potato, onion and milk into a saucepan and cook gently for about 20 minutes, until the potato is cooked. Cut the fish into chunks and add to the potato mixture. Cover and simmer for a further 20 minutes. Season to taste and add the butter just before serving.

Waxy potatoes. Serves 4.

A classic potato and fish soup which can be served as a main dish. The word 'skink' means 'broth' and this soup is traditionally thick, creamy and substantial enough to satisfy healthy appetites. I like to think that the American 'chowder' was derived from this very old recipe.

Coquille St Jacques
France

(see above)

225g (8oz) potato, mashed
8 medium scallops
4 scallop shells
275ml (10fl oz) milk
50g (2oz) butter
50g (2oz) flour
Salt and pepper to season
2 tbsp white wine

Pipe the mashed potato round the edge of the scallop shells to form a lip. Place under a grill and brown.

Gently poach the scallops in the milk for five minutes. Do not overcook. Drain the scallops and keep the milk. Melt the butter and stir in the flour and using the milk from the poached scallops, make a white sauce and season with salt and pepper. Add the white wine and cook gently until thickened. Continue cooking for a further 2 minutes, stirring constantly.

Place the scallops in the middle of the mashed potato and pour over a little of the sauce. Return to brown under a hot grill.

Floury potatoes. Serves 4.

Potato and prawn curry

1 tbsp ground cumin
1 tbsp ground coriander
2 tsp ground turmeric
1 tsp ground ginger
½ tsp chilli powder
Salt and freshly ground
    black pepper
2 tbsp wine vinegar
1 large onion, chopped
2 large cloves of garlic,
    crushed
2 tbsp vegetable oil
25g (1oz) butter
110g (4 oz) creamed coconut
    block
275ml (10fl oz) hot water
110g (4 oz) new potatoes,
    cooked and diced
450g (1 lb) prawns, peeled

Mix all the spices with the wine vinegar. Heat the oil and butter in a deep frying pan and gently cook the onion until golden brown. Stir in the spice mixture and crushed garlic and continue to cook for about 5 minutes.

Dissolve the creamed coconut in the hot water and, when dissolved, pour over the onion and spice mixture, stirring well, then allow to simmer for 10 minutes. Add the potatoes to the sauce, then carefully stir in the prawns and heat through. Season to taste. Serve with plain boiled rice.

New potatoes. Serves 4.

Fish stew

Finland

1.35kg (3 lb) trout, perch,
    pike or combination of all
6 large potatoes, peeled and
    diced
1 large onion, sliced
2 tsp salt
Good pinch allspice
900ml (1½ pt) water
1 fish stock cube
275ml (10fl oz) whipping
    cream
2 tbsp butter
Good pinch dill weed
Good grinding of black
    pepper

Remove any skin and bones from the fish and cut into 5cm (2in) pieces. In a large saucepan mix together the potatoes, onion, salt, allspice, water and fish stock cube. Cover and bring to a simmer over a medium heat and cook for about 15 minutes, or until the potatoes are tender.

Add the fish to the stew and cook for a further 15 minutes but do not allow to boil, as the fish should remain in pieces. When the fish is cooked add the cream, butter, dill and pepper.

Waxy or floury potatoes. Serves 6.

This is just one of many similar recipes from the northern area of Europe. It is simple to make and can be adapted to include any firm, white fish of your choice.

Potato, meat and pine nut rissoles

Greece

3 medium potatoes, cooked
450g (1 lb) minced beef
1 medium egg, beaten
50g (2oz) pine nuts
50g (2oz) currants
½ tsp thyme
½ tsp dill
½ tsp parsley
Salt and pepper to taste
Oil for frying

Mash potatoes thoroughly. Add the minced beef and beaten egg and mix well. Add the pine nuts, currants, herbs and seasoning and mix well.

Using wet hands, form the mixture into little, flat, round patties and fry in deep fat until brown.

Waxy potatoes. Serves 4.

Serve with home-made tomato sauce, or a salad of fresh tomatoes and chopped mint.

Potato and pepper scramble　　*Holland*

(see page 65 for illustration)

750g (1¾ lb) potatoes, cooked
  and peeled

100g (4 oz) streaky bacon,
  chopped

2 medium onions, peeled and
  diced

50g (2oz) butter

3 medium eggs

3 tbsp milk

1 green pepper, deseeded and
  diced

100g (4 oz) cooked ham,
  diced

Small pinch ground nutmeg

Salt and pepper to taste

1 tbsp chives, snipped for
  garnish

Cut cooked potatoes into thick slices. Fry bacon and onions in the butter until onions are transparent. Add the potato slices and cook until nicely browned.

Beat the eggs and add them to the milk, then mix together with the remaining ingredients. Pour over the potato mixture and cook gently until the egg has set. Do not stir. Serve hot, garnished with the chives.

Waxy or new potatoes. Serves 4.

Chicken and sweetcorn potato cakes　　*Canada*

200ml (7fl oz) milk

2 medium eggs

110g (4 oz) flour

Salt and pepper to taste

450g (1 lb) potatoes, peeled
  and grated

225g (8 oz) onion, thinly
  sliced

225g (8 oz) cooked chicken,
  finely chopped

200g (7oz) can sweetcorn,
  drained

25g (1oz) butter

Vegetable oil

Whisk the milk and eggs together, then beat in the flour and a pinch of salt until smooth. Chill in the refrigerator. Blanch the potatoes and onion together in a pan of boiling, salted water for 2 to 3 minutes. Drain well, pressing out as much liquid as possible.

Stir the chicken into the batter with the sweetcorn, potato and onion and season to taste. Heat the butter and a little oil in a frying pan. Spoon tablespoonfuls of the mixture into the pan, flatten and fry for about 4 minutes on each side. Drain on absorbent paper. Serve hot.

Floury potatoes. Makes 12.

This recipe uses up a little left-over chicken to make a very tasty supper dish.

Potato and ham dumplings　　*Austria*

225g (8 oz) rice

110g (4 oz) potatoes, cooked

110g (4 oz) lean ham, minced

25g (1oz) butter, melted

1 tsp parsley, chopped

Salt and pepper to taste

2 medium egg yolks

25g (1oz) flour

Oil for frying

Cook the rice until it is dry and fluffy. Put the potatoes through a ricer, or sieve. Mix with the rice, minced ham, melted butter, parsley and seasoning. Bind all ingredients together with the egg yolks.

Using floured hands, shape the mixture into small balls and fry in deep hot fat until nicely browned.

Floury potatoes. Makes 12.

These dumplings are a nice accompaniment to any soup.

Derry dumplings *Ireland*

900g (2 lb) cooked potatoes, mashed
2 tsp salt
Good grinding of black pepper
175g (6oz) pork chitterlings, cooked
50g (2oz) onion, grated
110g (4 oz) cheese, grated

Season the mashed potato with the salt and pepper. Using a potato scoop, form the potato into a ball. Make all the potato balls at one time and leave for the time being.

Cut the cooked chitterlings into small pieces and mix with the grated onion. Press a heaped teaspoonful into the centre of each potato ball and reshape. Roll each ball in the grated cheese and bake in the oven Gas mark 7, 425°F (220°C) until the cheese is golden and crunchy.

Floury potatoes. Serves 6.

This tasty supper dish is a useful way of using up pigs' chitterlings.

Aubergine and potato bake *Italy*

2 large aubergines, sliced
1 tsp salt
1 large onion, chopped
Oil for frying
400g (14oz) can of tomatoes
1 tsp oregano
Salt and pepper to taste
110g (4 oz) garlic sausage, sliced
450g (1 lb) potatoes, sliced
2 tomatoes, sliced
1 tbsp dry breadcrumbs
2 tbsp Parmesan cheese, grated

Put the sliced aubergines into a bowl and sprinkle with salt. Allow to stand for 30 minutes. Rinse and pat dry with kitchen paper. Fry the onion in 2 tbsp of oil until soft. Add the can of tomatoes, oregano and seasoning to taste. Cover and simmer gently for 20 minutes, then add the garlic sausage.

Fry the aubergines and potato slices separately in a frying pan with sufficient oil to stop them sticking to the pan. Put layers of aubergine, potato slices and tomato mixture into a greased casserole finishing with a layer of mixed aubergine and potatoes. Cover with fresh tomato slices, sprinkle with breadcrumbs and cheese. Bake in the oven Gas mark 4, 350°F (180°C) for 30 minutes, then brown under a hot grill.

Waxy potatoes. Serves 4.

I discovered this dish during my first visit to Turin. The recipe was given to me, with great gusto, by a large Italian lady who spoke very little English. I think I got it right, but it tastes delicious anyway!

Turkish lamb stew *Turkey*

900g (2 lb) lamb, cubed
450g (1 lb) potatoes, peeled and diced
4 tomatoes, peeled and sliced
4 onions, peeled and sliced
1 tsp sage, chopped
1 tsp fennel, chopped
1 tsp dill
2 bay leaves
1 green pepper, deseeded and diced
2 cloves of garlic
1.150 lt (2 pt) beef stock
Salt and pepper to taste

Place all the ingredients in a large pan. Bring to the boil, then allow to simmer for 2 hours.

Waxy potatoes. Serves 6.

Situated between Asia and Europe, Turkish recipes have developed as a marvellous mixture of both cuisines. The nomadic people from the past also left a legacy of easily cooked dishes.

Potato goulash

Germany

(see above)

1 kg (2¼ lb) potatoes, scrubbed

3 medium onions, peeled and chopped

50g (2oz) butter

50g (2oz) flour

600ml (1 pt) warm milk

450g (1 lb) Frankfurter sausages, sliced

3 tbsp parsley, chopped

4 tbsp pure apple juice

Salt and pepper to taste

Good pinch grated nutmeg

Cook the potatoes until just tender. Drain and peel while still warm. Cut into thick slices. Sauté the onions in the butter until just transparent. Add the flour and stir well. Gradually stir in the warm milk and bring to a simmer. Cook for about 4 minutes.

To this sauce add all the other ingredients, warming up again if necessary. Serve piping hot.

Waxy potatoes. Serves 4.

This recipe is not what I consider a traditional goulash, which is made with paprika for taste and colour. The addition of apple juice to the sauce gives this dish a piquant flavour. I have recommended Frankfurters as the meat content but you can use any German sausages.

Leeky potato frizzle

1.35kg (3 lb) breast of lamb
600ml (1 pt) beef stock
450g (1 lb) leeks
Salt and pepper to taste
700g (1½ lb) potatoes, mashed

Trim excess fat from the lamb and divide into single bones. Put into a saucepan with the stock and slowly bring to the boil, then cover and simmer for about 30 minutes.

While the lamb is cooking, trim and slice the leeks and cook in a pan with very little water for about 10 minutes. Drain the lamb and the leeks.

Season the potato and use like pastry to line a well-greased, shallow ovenproof dish. Spread the leeks over the potato and top with the lamb. Sprinkle on salt and pepper to taste and bake in the oven Gas mark 7, 425°F (220°C) for 30 minutes, until the lamb is brown and crisp.

Floury potatoes. Serves 6.

I like to serve this tasty supper dish with side dishes of pickled beetroot and red cabbage.

Brunswick stew

Germany

1 rabbit, jointed
Seasoned flour
Beef dripping
450g (1 lb) small new potatoes, with their skins on
1 medium tin of tomatoes
450g (1 lb) runner beans, stringed and sliced
4 spring onions, chopped
1 glass red wine
1 bay leaf
1 tsp dried thyme
Salt and pepper to taste

Toss the rabbit pieces in the seasoned flour and gently fry in the dripping until browned all over. Lift out of the fat and place in a casserole dish.

Add all the other ingredients to the casserole dish. Cover and cook in the oven Gas mark 4, 350°F (180°C) for 1½ hours.

New potatoes. Serves 4.

This wholesome and substantial stew does not require any finesse in the preparation.

Potato and bacon hotpot

Holland

700g (1½ lb) potatoes, peeled and sliced
225g (8oz) bacon
175g (6oz) Gouda cheese, grated
1 large onion, chopped
1 tbsp parsley, chopped
Salt and pepper to taste
25g (1oz) flour
150ml (5fl oz) vegetable or chicken stock
Parsley for garnish

Boil the potato slices in lightly salted water for 5 minutes, then drain well. Cut off the rind and chop the bacon. Reserve one-third of the cheese and layer the remainder in a greased casserole dish with the potatoes, bacon, onion and parsley. Sprinkle with salt and pepper.

Blend together the flour and stock until smooth, then pour over the casserole ingredients. Sprinkle with the rest of the cheese and cook in the oven Gas mark 4, 350°F (180°C) for 45 minutes. Serve garnished with parsley sprigs.

Waxy potatoes. Serves 4.

Puchero

900g (2 lb) beef, cut into 5cm (2in) pieces
1 boiling fowl, jointed
1 calf's foot, divided into 8 pieces
Boiling water
4 medium potatoes, peeled and sliced thickly
4 medium sweet potatoes, peeled and cubed
4 carrots, peeled and sliced
2 tomatoes, peeled and sliced
4 cobs of sweetcorn, halved
2 large onions, peeled and chopped
8 slices of liver sausage
8 thick rashers of bacon
8 pieces of pumpkin, about 7.5cm (3in) square
Salt and pepper to taste

Half fill a very large saucepan with water, bring to the boil and add a little salt. Put the beef, fowl and calf's foot into the boiling water and bring to a gentle simmer. Skim the surface and allow to cook for 1½ hours.

Add all the other ingredients and salt and pepper to taste. Add more water if necessary. Cook gently until the vegetables are tender.

Waxy potatoes. Serves 8.

As would be expected from the land of beef, I have discovered many unusual and highly-flavoured meat dishes. This traditional recipe uses sweet and ordinary potatoes and should be served as three separate dishes of meat, vegetables and broth.

Galician pote

1 shin of ham
450g (1 lb) oxtail
225g (8oz) white kidney beans, soaked in water for 12 hours
450g (1 lb) leg of pork meat
Cold water to cover
75g (3oz) chorizo sausage
1 small white cabbage
1.35 kg (3 lb) small potatoes
Salt to taste

Put the ham, oxtail, kidney beans and pork into a large saucepan and cover with cold water. bring to the boil, skim and allow to simmer for 2 hours.

Slice the chorizo and shred the cabbage, add to the meats and cook for a further 30 minutes. Add the small potatoes with their skins on and cook for a further 15 minutes or until the potatoes are tender. Season. Take out the meats and a few potatoes, mash and return to the liquid to thicken it.

New potatoes. Serves 8.

New potato and chicken casserole

225g (8oz) uncooked chicken meat
225g (8oz) lean bacon
450g (1 lb) new potatoes
3 medium onions
50g (2oz) butter
1 small carrot, diced
4 tbsp sweetcorn
1 large iceberg lettuce
Salt and freshly ground black pepper

Mince the chicken and bacon together. Peel and thinly slice the potatoes and onions. Shred the lettuce. Melt the butter in a frying pan and cook the onions until tender, but not browned. Add the carrot and the sweetcorn. Season to taste.

Butter an ovenproof dish and layer half each of the sliced potatoes, onions, carrots and sweetcorn then the shredded lettuce. Spread the chicken mixture over the top, then layer the other half of the vegetables, seasoning to taste. Cover the dish with buttered foil then bake in the oven Gas mark 4, 350°F (180°C) for 45 minutes. Finish by browning under a hot grill.

New potatoes. Serves 4.

Dublin coddle
Ireland

8 thick rashers of back bacon
8 large pork sausages
1.15 lt (2¼ pt) water
4 large onions, sliced
900g (2 lb) potatoes, sliced
Salt and pepper to taste
1 tbsp parsley, chopped
1 tbsp chives, chopped

Put the bacon, sausages and water into a saucepan, bring to the boil and cook for 5 minutes. Using a draining spoon, lift out the bacon and sausages and place in an ovenproof casserole dish, layering with slices of onion and potato. Season each layer with salt, pepper, parsley and chives, finishing with a layer of potato.

Add sufficient of the water to almost cover the top layer of potato. Put lid on casserole and cook in the oven Gas mark 3, 325°F (160°C) for 1 hour. Remove the lid and allow to cook for a further 30 minutes, or until the top is nicely browned.

Waxy potatoes. Serves 8.

This is a variation of the original recipe, using potato instead of oatmeal.

Sweet and savoury carbanado
Argentina

50g (2oz) butter
2 large onions, chopped
1 large tomato, peeled and sliced
700g (1½ lb) beef, minced
Salt and pepper to taste
275ml (10fl oz) beef stock
4 medium potatoes, peeled and cubed
6 plums, peeled and stoned
2 peaches, peeled, stoned and sliced
2 pears, peeled, cored and sliced
75g (3oz) seedless raisins

Melt the butter in a heavy casserole and fry the onions until brown. Add the sliced tomato and stir into the onions. Add the minced beef and brown for a few minutes. Add seasoning and stock.

Cover the casserole and cook very gently, either in the oven or on top of the cooker for 1 hour. Add the potatoes and fresh fruit and cook until the potatoes are just tender. A few minutes before serving, add the raisins.

Waxy potatoes. Serves 8.

The Argentinians, like the Germans, greatly enjoy sweet and savoury ingredients together. This recipe is a typical combination.

Beef casserole with potatoes
Australia
(Wahgunyah steak)

1 apple
1 onion
2 stalks celery
25g (1oz) cooking fat or oil
450g (16oz) cooked braising steak
3 tbsp tomato purée
1 tbsp Worcestershire sauce
275ml (10fl oz) brown stock
225g (8oz) cooked potato, mashed
50g (2oz) butter
Salt and pepper to taste

Peel and core the apple and slice with the onion and celery. Sauté the mixture in the fat until golden brown. Add the cooked steak, purée, Worcestershire sauce and stock and bring to a gentle simmer. Cook for 10 minutes.

Beat the mashed potato with butter and pipe a border round a serving dish. Pile the casserole mixture in the middle of the potato and brown in a hot oven.

Floury potatoes. Serves 4.

The culinary traditions of Australia come, in fact, from New Zealand and are based on the mother country, Great Britain. The main difference in diet is that the antipodeans eat much more meat and less starch. I have, however, found several Australian dishes which do use potatoes.

Casserole of lamb with potatoes and gin   *Holland*

4 tbsp vegetable oil

1 large onion, peeled and chopped

225g (8oz) red cabbage, shredded

2 tbsp flour

1 tsp paprika

Salt and freshly ground black pepper

450g (1 lb) lamb, cut into small cubes

3 tbsp gin, Dutch Genève if available

2 tbsp lime or lemon juice

700g (1½ lb) potatoes, diced

600ml (1 pt) stock

2 bay leaves

50g (2oz) butter

1 tbsp parsley, finely chopped

2 medium cloves of garlic, crushed

Heat 2 tsp of the vegetable oil in a deep frying pan and gently cook the onion until transparent. Add the cabbage and, stirring occasionally allow to cook for 5 minutes until the oil is absorbed.

Heat the remaining oil in a heavy casserole dish. Mix together the flour, paprika, salt and pepper and coat the meat, then brown on all sides in the hot oil. Pour in the gin, shake well and set the gin alight. Shake again until the flames die down, then pour in the lime or lemon juice. Add the onions and cabbage, the diced potatoes and sufficient stock to just cover the ingredients. Season to taste and add the bay leaves.

Cover and cook in the oven Gas mark 4, 350°F (180°C) for 1 hour or until the lamb is tender. Mix together the butter, chopped parsley and crushed garlic. Stir into the casserole just before serving.

Waxy potatoes. Serves 6.

Iranian lamb and potatoes   *Iran*

175g (6oz) onions

450g (1 lb) tomatoes

700g (1½ lb) shoulder of lamb, boned

1 tbsp oil

2 cloves of garlic, crushed

Salt to taste

Pinch each of cayenne pepper and saffron

1 bouquet garni

225g (8oz) marrow

700g (1½ lb) potatoes, peeled and quartered

110g (4 oz) onion as garnish

25g (1oz) flour

55ml (2fl oz) milk

2 tbsp parsley, chopped

Finely dice 175g (6oz) of onions, skin, deseed and coarsely chop the tomatoes. Cut the meat into 12 pieces and brown in hot oil in a casserole dish. Stirring well, drain off the fat, then add the onion and cook gently without browning. Add the chopped tomatoes and crushed garlic, cover and leave to simmer for 5 minutes. Pour over sufficient water to just cover. Season with salt, cayenne pepper and saffron, then add the bouquet garni. Bring to the boil and skim if necessary. Reduce heat and allow to simmer for about 45 minutes.

Cut the unskinned marrow into rings then into four pieces, add to the potatoes. Add the marrow and potatoes to the casserole and cook for a further 20 minutes.

Slice the 110g (4 oz) of onions into rings, dip in the milk then in the flour and fry in 1 tbsp hot oil until golden brown. Use these rings and a sprinkling of chopped parsley to garnish the casserole.

Waxy potatoes. Serves 6.

Greece

Stuffed peppers
(see opposite)

4 peppers, red or green
225g (8 oz) cooked, sieved
potatoes
175g (6oz) ham, finely
chopped
25g (1oz) butter, melted
1 medium egg, beaten
50g (2oz) mushrooms,
chopped
1 tbsp parsley, chopped
Salt and pepper to taste

Blanch the peppers, remove stalks and seeds and cut a lid from the top of each. Combine all the stuffing ingredients and fill each pepper. Replace the lids and put in an ovenproof dish. Pour a little water into the dish. Cover and bake at Gas mark 5, 375°F (190°C) for 35 minutes.

Floury potatoes.
Serves 4.

I serve this dish with freshly baked crusty rolls and a greek salad of feta cheese, tomatoes and black olives. Dress the salad with a little olive oil.

Lincolnshire pork casserole　　　*England*

1 shallot, chopped
1 clove of garlic, crushed
150ml (5fl oz) white wine
1 tbsp cider vinegar
2 bay leaves
Small bunch of parsley
Sprig each of thyme and
　marjoram
1 tbsp gin, optional
Salt and freshly ground black
　pepper

Marinade: combine all the ingredients, pour over the pork chops and allow to stand for 24 hours.

4 large pork spare ribs, or
　pork chops
1 tbsp vegetable oil
1 large onion, chopped
700g (1½ lb) potatoes, peeled
　and sliced
6 rashers streaky bacon,
　without rind
2 large leeks, chopped
2 tbsp parsley, finely chopped

Casserole: lift chops out of the marinade and brown in heated oil. Put about half the quantities of each of the onions, potatoes, small pieces of bacon and chopped leeks in layers in an ovenproof dish. Add the browned chops, then top with the remaining vegetables.

Strain the marinade over the casserole, cover the dish and bake in the oven Gas mark 3, 325°F (160°C) for about 2 hours. Remove the lid and drain off as much fat as possible. Serve garnished with chopped parsley.

Waxy potatoes. Serves 4.

Mixed meats with olives, raisins and potatoes　　　*Mexico*

(see front cover for illustration)

110g (4 oz) beef, minced
110g (4 oz) pork, minced
3 tsp wine vinegar
½ tsp salt
Good grinding of black
　pepper
½ tsp brown sugar
1 tbsp cooking oil
1 small onion, finely grated
1 clove of garlic, crushed
1 green chilli, chopped
1 red pepper, deseeded
　and sliced
2 sticks of celery, finely
　chopped
1 beef stock cube
2 medium potatoes, peeled,
　cooked and cubed
12 stuffed olives, sliced
1 tbsp flaked almonds
1 tbsp raisins
400g (14oz) tin of peeled
　tomatoes
1 tbsp tomato purée

Mix the minced beef and pork together with the vinegar, salt, pepper and sugar. Heat the oil and gently fry the onion, garlic, chilli, pepper and celery for 5 minutes. Add the meat and stir over a fairly high heat for about 10 minutes until well browned. Drain off as much surplus oil as possible, taking care to retain the meat juices.

Add all the remaining ingredients and cook gently for about 15 to 20 minutes, stirring occasionally until the liquids have been absorbed and the meat has dried out a little.

Waxy potatoes. Serves 4.

This recipe is one of the most popular ways of cooking minced meat in Mexico. It can be used as a filling, or served with rice as a light lunch dish.

Savoury potato nests *Australia*

(see above)

1.75 kg (4 lb) potatoes, peeled
110g (4 oz) butter
2 medium eggs
Salt and pepper
450g (1 lb) minced cooked
**   beef with onions**
50g (2oz) peanuts, chopped
Parsley, chopped

Cook the potatoes in lightly salted water until tender. Drain and mash well with the butter. Beat in the eggs and seasoning.

Put the potato mixture into a piping bag fitted with a star nozzle. Pipe out four flat circles about 10cm (4in) diameter on a baking tray lined with non-stick paper. Pipe another circle around the edges to make nests. Divide the mince into each nest. Garnish with the peanuts and parsley.

If serving immediately, brush the potato with a little beaten egg and brown under the grill. Serve hot.

Floury potatoes. Serves 6.

This recipe is the ideal convenience dish and can be prepared in advance, frozen and cooked in a microwave oven when required.

Potatoes with cheesy bacon

Yugoslavia

900g (2 lb) potatoes
2 tbsp fresh brown
   breadcrumbs
110g (4 oz) butter
225g (8oz) cottage cheese
175g (6oz) smoked back
   bacon, grilled until crisp
2 tsp salt
Good grinding of black
   pepper

Boil the potatoes in their skins until tender. Peel and slice. Grease a shallow casserole dish and coat with some of the breadcrumbs. Melt the butter and cheese together. Layer the casserole with potato slices, some crisp bacon and half the cheese mixture. Repeat, and sprinkle the remainder of the breadcrumbs on top seasoning to taste.

Bake uncovered in the oven Gas mark 5, 375°F (190°C) for about 1 hour. To serve, place a large plate over the casserole dish right side down, turn the dish upside down.

Waxy or floury potatoes. Serves 6.

This is a favourite luncheon or supper dish and so easy to prepare.

Chicken and egg pie with meatballs

U.S.A.

225g (8oz) cooked chicken
   meat
225g (8oz) sausage meat,
   rolled into tiny balls
4 medium eggs, hard-boiled
110g (4 oz) button mushrooms
2 tbsp fresh parsley, chopped
Salt and pepper to taste
275ml (10fl oz) chicken stock
   or cold milk
50g (2oz) cornflour
225g (8 oz) potato puff
   pastry, see page 140

Grease a suitable pie dish and place a pie funnel in the centre. Place the chicken and small meatballs in the bottom. Shell and slice the eggs and place on top of the mixture. Scatter the button mushrooms and parsley over the top and season with salt and pepper.

Thicken the chicken stock or milk with the cornflour and pour over the ingredients. Cover the pie dish with puff pastry, brush with cold milk and bake in the oven Gas mark 4, 350°F (180°C) for 40 minutes.

Floury potatoes. Serves 6.

This 'cute little recipe' was given to me by an American lady, temporarily living in the United Kingdom. She was a frequent visitor to my restaurant and passed on to me several of her family recipes.

Old Kentish shepherd's pie

England

25g (1oz) butter
1 large onion, finely chopped
1 tsp thyme, chopped
1 tbsp parsley, chopped
450g (1 lb) cooked lamb,
   minced
275ml (10fl oz) thick, brown
   gravy
Salt and freshly ground black
   pepper
700g (1½ lb) potatoes,
   mashed

Melt the butter and gently fry the onion until soft. Add the thyme, parsley, minced lamb, gravy and seasoning and put into an ovenproof casserole dish.

Top with the mashed potato, roughing up the surface with a fork, and bake in the oven Gas mark 4, 350°F (180°C) for 50 minutes, or until the top is nicely browned.

Floury potatoes. Serves 6.

This dish is a well-tried family favourite and so simple to prepare. Serve with buttered cabbage and buttered swede, mashed and seasoned with white pepper.

Shropshire fidget pie
England

450g (1 lb) potatoes, peeled and cut into 6mm (¼in) slices

225g (8oz) cooking apples, peeled, cored and sliced

225g (8oz) streaky bacon, cut into small pieces

1 tbsp Muscovado sugar

150ml (5fl oz) meat stock

Salt and pepper to taste

225g (8oz) potato puff pastry, see page 140

Cold milk

Put a pie funnel in the middle of a suitable dish. Arrange layers of potato, apple and bacon around it. Sprinkle on the sugar, salt and pepper. Pour over the meat stock.

Cover with the pastry and cut the trimmings into suitable shapes for a garnish. Brush with cold milk and bake in the oven Gas mark 4, 350°F (180°C) for about 90 minutes, until the pastry is well-risen and golden brown.

Waxy potatoes. Serves 6.

There are many different recipes for 'fidget pie' but this is my favourite. It is a very popular local bar snack, served with crusty bread and butter.

Beef, beer and potato pie
Belgium

450g (1 lb) braising steak, cubed

2 tbsp oil

1 large onion, sliced

275ml (10fl oz) strong beer, hot

150ml (5fl oz) beef stock, hot

450g (1 lb) new potatoes, left in their jackets or scraped

175g (6oz) button mushrooms

Salt and pepper to taste

2 tbsp parsley, chopped

225g (8oz) potato puff pastry, see page 140

Cold milk

Heat the oil and brown the cubed braising steak. Remove the steak but keep warm. Fry the sliced onion until lightly browned. Add the steak to the onion, pour over the hot beer and stock. Cook for about 45 minutes. Add the new potatoes, button mushrooms and parsley, season to taste and cook for a further 10 minutes. Leave to cool.

When cold put the mixture in a pie dish, with a pie funnel placed in the centre. Cover with the pastry and cut the trimmings into suitable shapes for a garnish. Brush with cold milk and bake in the oven Gas mark 4, 350°F (180°C) for 45 minutes.

New potatoes. Serves 4.

This appetising supper dish can be prepared the previous day. Leave it in the refrigerator until required, then brush with milk and bake as given above. It is traditionally served with a dish of red cabbage cooked with apples.

Oven cooked potatoes with bacon
France

1 kg (2lb 2oz) potatoes, sliced

3 cloves of garlic, crushed

1 bayleaf, broken into four

Salt and black pepper to taste

175g (6oz) streaky bacon

Boiling water to cover

Layer the thinly sliced potatoes in a suitable ovenproof dish with the garlic, bayleaf and seasoning. Fry the bacon until crisp and break into small pieces. Scatter the bacon and dribble the fat all over the potatoes.

Cover with water that is almost, but not quite, boiling. Bake in the oven Gas mark 7, 425°F (220°C) for 1 hour, until the potatoes are tender.

Waxy potatoes. Serves 6.

This is a warming winter dish from the mountain region of the Auvergne and was originally cooked in the local baker's oven.

Chilli and red cabbage with savoury potato topping

Argentina

3 tbsp olive or vegetable oil

450g (1 lb) minced lamb or beef, can be leftovers

2 large onions

3 medium cloves of garlic

1 green pepper

1 green chilli pepper

2 tsp chilli powder

Salt and freshly ground black pepper

2 tbsp tomato purée

150ml (5fl oz) red wine or stock

1 medium tin of tomatoes

1 small red cabbage

225g (8oz) creamed potatoes

175g (6oz) leeks, chopped and sweated in butter

1 tbsp fresh breadcrumbs

25g (1oz) butter

Heat the oil in a large saucepan. Add the meat and fry until brown all over. Meanwhile, peel and chop the onions and garlic, remove the seeds and core from the green chilli and pepper, chop the flesh finely and mix all together with the browned meat. Stir well over a low heat until the onion looks transparent, then add the chilli powder, salt and pepper, tomato purée, wine or stock and the tinned tomatoes. Cover the saucepan with a lid and continue to cook until still moist but with not too much liquid.

Shred the cabbage and blanch in boiling salted water for 5 minutes, then drain thoroughly. Arrange one-third of the cabbage in a deep oven-proof dish, cover with half the meat, repeat these 2 layers again and finish with a layer of cabbage.

Mix together the creamed potatoes and leeks and carefully spread over the top of the meat and cabbage, forking to leave a rough surface. Sprinkle with breadcrumbs and dot with small pieces of butter. Bake in the oven Gas mark 4, 350°F (180°C) for 1 hour, or until thoroughly heated through and nicely browned.

Floury potatoes. Serves 8.

Potato, chicken and sweetcorn aspic

Canada

(see opposite)

1 lt (1¾ pt) aspic

450g (1 lb) new potatoes, cooked and diced

50g (2oz) sweetcorn

50g (2oz) green peas

225g (8oz) chicken, cooked and cubed

75ml (3fl oz) mayonnaise

75ml (3fl oz) cider vinegar

Salt and pepper to season

Watercress for garnish

Dissolve the aspic as given on the packet and pour a little into a suitable ring mould to a depth of about 2.5cm (1in) and chill this until set, about 10 minutes. Keep the remaining aspic liquid warm.

Mix together the potatoes, sweetcorn, peas and cubed chicken with the mayonnaise, cider vinegar and season with the salt and pepper.

When the aspic in the ring mould has set, pile the vegetable and chicken mixture on top, then pour over the remaining aspic liquid and again chill in the refrigerator until set.

To serve, carefully immerse the outside of the mould in hot water to loosen the salad. Put a plate on top of the mould and turn upside down. Garnish with watercress and serve with a crisp lettuce, pepper and pineapple salad.

New potatoes. Serves 6.

Baked potatoes

The humble jacket potato has come a long way from its original purpose of making any available meat go further, and to help stave off hunger pangs. As the first method of cooking meat was a form of barbecue over an open fire, it is probable that potatoes were placed in the hot embers to bake. Personally, I still think they taste delicious straight from the ashes! Today this dish is regarded as a sophisticated snack, or main meal, and can be topped with an endless variety of sauces, or served with the flesh scooped out and combined with other savoury ingredients.

Baked potatoes take rather a long time to cook in a conventional cooker, so it is well worth putting a couple of extra potatoes in whenever you use the oven for any purpose, as these can easily be re-heated. When required, simply brush them with a little melted butter or vegetable oil and bake in the oven Gas mark 7, 425°F (220°C) for about 15 minutes, or until the skin is crisp and the flesh piping hot. You can also use them up in recipes which need cooked potatoes.

I prefer not to wrap the potatoes in foil, as I think the crispness of the skin complements the soft, floury texture of the flesh, but this is a matter of choice. It is also important not to place the potatoes on a tray, or let them touch any part of the oven in cooking, as this will make the skin soft. It is well worth investing in a jacket potato rack, which will enable you to cook several potatoes at a time.

One of the best ways of retaining the nutritional value of the potato is to cook it in its jacket without water and, with the arrival of the microwave method of cooking, this can now be achieved in a matter of minutes, instead of more than an hour in a conventional oven. However, the skin does not have that traditional crisp texture.

Baked potatoes are tasty and filling served plain or just split open and topped with butter or grated cheese. If you want to fill the potato, however, cut off the top and carefully scoop out the flesh while it is still hot, then mix with butter, mayonnaise, or any other combination of savoury ingredients.

*opposite: see page 105 for turkey and ham topping recipe, (top right);
page 106 for liver, mushroom and onion filling, (bottom left);
page 106 for beef and mushroom filling, (bottom right);
and page 106 for smoked ham and pineapple topping, (top left).*

Baked potatoes

2 large potatoes, scrubbed
but not peeled
1 tsp vegetable oil

Prick the washed potatoes all over with a fork, then coat with a little oil to give a shiny skin.

To cook in a conventional oven, heat the oven Gas mark 7, 425°F (220°C). Place in a potato rack and bake for about 1½ hours, or until the insides are tender and the skin crisp.

To cook by the microwave method, follow the instructions given in the manual.

Floury potatoes. Serves 2 or 4. Vegetarian dish.

If you feel it is extravagant to heat the oven just to bake potatoes, try par-boiling them whole in their skins for about 20 minutes, then follow the method above and bake in the oven for about 15 minutes.

Potato Chantilly

France

2 large baked potatoes
150ml (5fl oz) double cream
1 tbsp potato, cooked and
mashed
1 tsp mustard powder
1 tbsp wine vinegar
½ tsp salt
Good grinding of black
pepper
Fresh parsley, chopped for
garnish

Whip the cream until stiff then carefully fold in all the other ingredients.

Split the baked potatoes and pour the sauce over. Alternatively, scoop out the flesh and mix with the sauce. Then arrange the mixture back in the shells and place under a hot grill until lightly browned on top. Garnish with chopped parsley.

Floury potatoes. Serves 4. Vegetarian dish.

Sour cream sauce

Luxembourg

2 large baked potatoes
75g (3oz) sour cream
2 medium eggs, hard-boiled
1 tbsp wine vinegar
½ tsp caster sugar
½ tsp salt
Good grinding of black
pepper

Rub the hard-boiled eggs through a sieve and add to the sour cream. Gradually thin down with the vinegar and stir in the sugar, salt and pepper.

Split the baked potatoes and pour the sauce over. Alternatively, scoop out the flesh and mix with the sauce then arrange the mixture back in the shells and place under a hot grill until lightly browned on top.

Floury potatoes. Serves 4.

Horseradish sauce

England

2 large baked potatoes
150ml (5fl oz) double cream
4 tbsp mayonnaise
2 tbsp horseradish, grated
1 tsp mustard powder
½ tsp salt
Paprika for garnish

Beat the cream until thickened, fold in all the other ingredients except the paprika.

Scoop out the flesh from the four baked potato halves and mix well with the horseradish sauce. Return the mixture to the shells and garnish with a sprinkling of paprika. Warm through in a hot oven.

Floury potatoes. Serves 4. Vegetarian dish.

Tangy orange sauce
U.S.A.

2 large baked potatoes
600ml (1 pt) good brown
  gravy
1 tbsp thick orange
  marmalade
1 tbsp sherry

Whisk all ingredients together. Split the baked potato and pour the sauce over. Alternatively, scoop out the flesh and mix with the sauce. Then arrange the mixture back in the shells and place under a hot grill until lightly browned on top.

Floury potatoes. Serves 4. Vegetarian dish.

Cream cheese and spring onion filling
Scotland

2 large baked potatoes
225 (8oz) full cream cheese
110g (4 oz) spring onions,
  chopped
1 tbsp parsley, chopped
1 tsp lemon juice
3 tbsp cream or top of the
  milk
Salt and black pepper to taste

Halve the baked potatoes and scoop out the flesh. Mash the flesh thoroughly and mix with all the other ingredients. Fill the potato shells with this mixture and place in a hot oven to heat through.

Floury potatoes. Serves 4. Vegetarian dish.

Sour cream and Parmesan filling
U.S.A.

2 large baked potatoes
4 tbsp sour cream
6 tbsp whipping cream
2 tbsp Parmesan cheese
Salt and black pepper to taste
1 tbsp chives, chopped
1 tbsp parsley, chopped
2 tbsp almond flakes
Good sprinkling of paprika

Halve the baked potatoes and scoop out the flesh. Mash the flesh thoroughly with the sour cream and the whipped up cream. Stir in the Parmesan cheese and all other ingredients except the almonds and paprika. Use these to garnish the potato mixture when you have filled the shells.

Floury potatoes. Serves 4. Vegetarian dish.

Lemon and chutney filling
England

2 large baked potatoes
3 tbsp mango chutney
1 tbsp lemon juice
1 tbsp butter
Good grinding of black
pepper

Halve the baked potatoes and scoop out the flesh. Put all the other ingredients into a saucepan and heat gently until the butter has melted, stirring constantly.

Mix together the potato flesh which has been mashed with the chutney mixture and pile all back into the potato skins. Place under a hot grill until nicely browned on top.

Floury potatoes. Serves 4. Vegetarian dish.

Pineapple yogurt and cheese filling　　*Canada*

2 large baked potatoes
Two 110g (4oz) cartons
　pineapple yogurt
175g (6oz) strong cheese,
　grated
1 tbsp parsley, chopped
75g (3oz) cheese, grated for
　garnish

Halve the potatoes and scoop out the flesh. Mash the potato flesh and mix thoroughly with the pineapple yogurt, 175g (6oz) cheese and the parsley. Pile this mixture back into the potato shells and top with the remaining grated cheese. Bake in a hot oven until heated through and golden brown on top.

Floury potatoes. Serves 4. Vegetarian dish.

Boozy prawn and pepper topping　　*England*
(see below)

2 large baked potatoes
450g (1 lb) prawns, cooked
　and peeled
110g (4oz) thick cream
2 tbsp tomato sauce or
　ketchup
1 tbsp whisky
Few drops of tabasco sauce
Pinch salt
Good grinding black pepper
1 tbsp green peas
2 tbsp spring onions, chopped
Green part of spring onion
　for garnish

Mix all the ingredients together and pile on top of the halved baked potatoes. Garnish with strips of spring onion and and a few of the prawns.

Floury potatoes. Serves 4.

Tuna and potato filling
U.S.A.

2 large baked potatoes

200g (7oz) can tuna fish, flaked

25g (1oz) butter

4 tbsp sour cream

Salt and black pepper to taste

110g (4 oz) streaky bacon, grilled until crisp, crumbled

Halve the baked potatoes and scoop out the flesh leaving a thin shell. Mash the potato flesh thoroughly and mix with all the other ingredients. Spoon the mixture back into the potato shells and mark the surface with a fork. Place in a hot oven and bake until warmed through and slightly browned on top.

Floury potatoes. Serves 4.

Turkey and broccoli topping
England

2 large baked potatoes

275g (10oz) broccoli, cooked and chopped

175g (6 oz) turkey, cooked, can be leftovers

4 tsp cornflour

110ml (4fl oz) milk

Salt and pepper to taste

Pinch of mustard powder

Pinch of paprika

½ chicken stock cube

2 slices of processed cheese, in strips

Red pepper slices for garnish

Halve the baked potatoes and score the tops with a fork. Cut the turkey into cubes and mix with the broccoli in a basin. Mix the cornflour with the milk, then add the salt, pepper, mustard, paprika and chicken stock cube. Cook the cornflour mix on a fairly low heat until the stock cube is dissolved and the mixture has thickened. Pour the sauce over the turkey and broccoli and mix well.

Carefully spoon the mixture on top of the baked potatoes, garnish with the cheese strips and pepper slices and grill until the cheese has melted.

Floury potatoes. Serves 4.

Turkey and ham topping
U.S.A.

(see page 101, top right, for illustration)

2 large baked potatoes

110g (4oz) cooked turkey meat

110g (4oz) cooked ham

1 tbsp green peas

4 tbsp mayonnaise

Salt and pepper to taste

Rolls of sliced ham for garnish

Sprig of watercress for garnish

Halve the baked potatoes and from each scoop out about 1 tbsp of flesh. Dice the cooked turkey and ham and add to the potato flesh which has been mashed. Stir in the peas and mayonnaise. Season to taste. Pile back into the skins. Garnish with small rolls of sliced ham and watercress.

Floury potatoes. Serves 4.

Liver, mushroom and onion filling

Scotland

(see page 101, bottom left, for illustration)

2 large baked potatoes
1 medium onion, sliced in
  rings
110g (4oz) button mushrooms
110g (4oz) lambs' liver in
  strips
Oil for frying
Salt and pepper
Parsley for garnish

Halve the baked potatoes and scoop out the flesh. Sauté the onion rings, button mushrooms and liver in a little oil until the liver is cooked. Mix with the potato flesh and pile back into the potato skins. Garnish with the parsley.

Floury potatoes. Serves 4.

Beef and mushroom filling with horseradish

England

(see page 101, bottom right, for illustration)

2 large baked potatoes
110g (4oz) mushrooms
1 medium onion, diced
225g (8oz) beef, in thin strips
1 tbsp horseradish sauce
Salt and pepper
Parsley for garnish

Halve the baked potatoes and scoop out the flesh. Lightly fry the mushrooms and diced onion and keep hot while you fry the beef until cooked. Mix the potato flesh with the beef, mushrooms and onion, then stir in the horseradish sauce and season to taste. Pile back into the skins. Garnish with the parsley.

Floury potatoes. Serves 4.

Hot dog and sweetcorn filling

U.S.A.

2 large baked potatoes
110g (4 oz) hot-dog sausages,
  sliced
200g (7oz) can sweetcorn,
  cream style
Salt and good grinding black
  pepper
110g (4oz) strong cheese,
  grated for garnish

Halve the baked potatoes and scoop out the flesh. Mash the flesh thoroughly then mix in all ingredients except the grated cheese. Pile this mixture into the potato shells and top with the grated cheese. Place in a hot oven to heat through and until the cheese has browned on top.

Floury potatoes. Serves 4.

Smoked ham and pineapple topping

Holland

(see page 101, top left, for illustration)

2 large baked potatoes
225g (8oz) smoked ham
110g (4oz) cheese
2 slices pineapple, chopped
3 tbsp mayonnaise
4 slices pineapple, grilled
  and halved
Watercress for garnish

Halve the baked potatoes and score the tops with a fork. Dice the ham. Grate the cheese and mix the ham, cheese and chopped pineapple with the mayonnaise. Pile the mixture on top of the baked potato halves. Garnish with the grilled pineapple and the watercress.

Floury potatoes. Serves 4.

Bacon and sweetcorn filling U.S.A.
(see above, left)

2 large baked potatoes

225g (8oz) streaky smoked
  bacon

6 tbsp sweetcorn, tinned

110g (4oz) butter

Grinding of black pepper

4 extra slices of streaky
  bacon, grilled, for garnish

Halve the baked potatoes and scoop out the flesh. Grill the bacon till crisp, including the extra slices. Cut the 225g (8oz) of bacon into small pieces and mix with the potato, sweetcorn, butter and pepper. Pile the mixture back into the potato shells and garnish with the remaining grilled bacon.

Floury potatoes. Serves 4.

Savoury minced beef and tomato filling *England*
(see above, right)

2 large baked potatoes

110g (4oz) minced beef

1 medium onion

1 tbsp tomato purée

Salt and pepper

Fresh tomato slices for
  garnish

Halve the baked potatoes and scoop out the flesh. Cook together the minced beef, onion and tomato purée and season with the salt and pepper. When thoroughly cooked, mix with the potato flesh and pile back into the potato skins. Garnish with fresh tomato slices.

Floury potatoes. Serves 4.

Sweet potatoes

The *Impomoea Batatas*, or sweet potato, was brought to Spain by Columbus when he returned from his epic voyage to Hispaniola in 1492, but it was not until the sixteenth century that the potato was cultivated in limited areas. Columbus is reported to have said that the potatoes 'looked like yams but tasted like chestnuts'. During the fourteenth and fifteenth centuries, various European explorers give accounts of these strange roots which had reached America, via the Marquesas Islands, from Peru.

One island where the sweet potato was grown as a normal crop was Martinique, the birthplace of Marie-Josephe-Rase Detascher, who later changed her name to 'Josephine' and became the wife of Napolean Bonaparte. She helped to make the plant popular in France, just as she did with many other exotic tropical plants. By chance, the women of the Court also took a hand in introducing the sweet potato! They were so jealous of Josephine and enraged that a Creole should become Empress that they spread abroad the belief that the plant was, in fact, an aphrodisiac. The courtesans of the day, who wanted to titillate their jaded patrons, created a steady market by feeding their clients with slices of sweet potatoes, boiled, skinned and then dipped in fresh orange juice and coated with sugar.

The sweet potato eventually reached England from Spain and was sold in the streets of London in almost the same way as chestnuts are roasted and sold today. Because of the belief in their attributed aphrodisiac qualities, however, they were rather expensive and did not form part of the everyday diet of the working population.

As their name implies, sweet potatoes contain more fat and sugar than ordinary potatoes and are therefore mainly used for puddings. The recipes given in this section come from as far afield as New Zealand and Bermuda and I hope you will be encouraged to introduce this delicacy to your family.

Opposite: see page 110 for
Sweet mashed potatoes recipe, left,
and page 111 for
Candied sweet potatoes, right.

Sweet mashed potatoes U.S.A.

4 medium sweet potatoes
110g (4oz) butter
½ tsp salt
4 tbsp fresh orange juice
1 tbsp grated orange peel

Boil potatoes and while still hot pass through a sieve or ricer or mash. Add all other ingredients and beat until light and fluffy.

Sweet potatoes. Serves 4. Vegetarian dish.

The combination of sweet potato and orange has been a favourite since Elizabethan times, but for a savoury flavour substitute the orange with a few grains of grated nutmeg, allspice and cinnamon.

Sweet potatoes with cinnamon and orange Bermuda

900g (2 lb) sweet potatoes, peeled
1 orange
½ lemon
110g (4oz) dark brown sugar
75g (3oz) butter
55ml (2fl oz) tepid water
Cinnamon powder

Cut potatoes into about 1cm (½in) squares. Slice orange and lemon as thinly as possible and arrange potatoes and fruit in layers in a buttered ovenproof dish. Sprinkle with sugar and dab small pieces of butter all over.

Add the water, then cover with a lid or foil and bake in the oven Gas mark 4, 350°F (180°C) for 1 hour. Dust the top with the cinnamon and continue baking uncovered for a further 15 minutes.

Sweet potatoes. Serves 6. Vegetarian dish.

Sweet potato purée Mexico

450g (1 lb) sweet potato
600ml (1 pt) water
75g (3oz) butter
1 tsp baking powder
150ml (5fl oz) double cream
1 tbsp breadcrumbs

Boil the potatoes in their skins in the water for about 35 minutes or until tender. Peel and while still hot, mash to a purée with the butter. Stir in the baking powder and cream.

Turn into a well-greased shallow casserole dish and bake in the oven at Gas mark 4, 350°F (180°C) for 25 minutes. Sprinkle with the breadcrumbs and place under a hot grill to brown.

Sweet potatoes. Serves 4. Vegetarian dish.

It is customary to eat sweet potato in America as part of a Thanksgiving dinner. The sweet potato is also popular in Mexico, either as a vegetable or as a pudding, when sugar would be added to it. This recipe is for a side dish to accompany a main course.

Sweet potato Imperiale Jamaica

225g (8oz) sweet potatoes, peeled and sliced
175g (6oz) cooking apples, peeled and grated
3 medium bananas, sliced
Salt and pepper to taste
1 tsp paprika
25g (1oz) butter
150ml (5fl oz) apricots, sieved

Mix together the sliced potatoes, grated apples, sliced bananas, salt, pepper and paprika.

Put the mixture into a well-greased casserole dish, dot with the butter and bake in a moderate oven Gas mark 3, 325°F (170°C) for 1 hour.

Remove from the oven and spread over the apricot purée.

Sweet potatoes. Serves 4. Vegetarian dish.

Serve as an accompaniment to any roast or cold meats.

Candied sweet potatoes

New Zealand

(see page 109 for illustration)

450g (1 lb) sweet potatoes, peeled and thickly sliced

110g (4oz) fresh apricots, cooked and drained

75g (3oz) brown sugar

50g (2oz) butter, melted

55ml (2fl oz) liquid from the cooked apricots

1 tsp grated rind of an orange

1 tsp grated rind of a lemon

Line a casserole dish with a layer of sliced potatoes and cover with a layer of apricots. Sprinkle some of the brown sugar over the apricots and repeat the layers, finishing with sweet potatoes. Mix the melted butter, lemon rind and orange rind and pour over the mixture.

Bake uncovered for 45 minutes in the oven Gas mark 6, 400°F (200°C), basting once or twice during cooking with a little more melted butter. Serve hot or cold with whipped cream.

Sweet potatoes. Serves 6. Vegetarian dish.

This delicious recipe is a traditional Maori dish.

Sweet potatoes candied Jamaican-style

Jamaica

700g (1½ lb) sweet potatoes

75ml (3fl oz) lime juice

225ml (8fl oz) golden syrup

175g (6oz) dark brown sugar

330ml (12fl oz) hot water

Use small potatoes for this recipe

Peel and divide potatoes into four lengthwise, then blanch in boiling water for about 12 minutes. Drain, pat dry and place in a deep-sided roasting tin. Make a syrup by blending all the other ingredients together.

Pour over the potatoes and bake in the oven Gas mark 5, 375°F (190°C) until golden brown and candied. Baste several times during cooking.

Sweet potatoes. Serves 4. Vegetarian dish.

This recipe is from Jamaica where sweet potato recipes are a speciality and have been popular for many years.

Sweet potato pone

Jamaica

1 coconut, grated, and milk reserved

900ml (1½ pt) hot water

700g (1½ lb) uncooked sweet potato, peeled

150g (5oz) dark brown sugar

150g (5oz) raisins

25g (1oz) currants

1 tsp cinnamon powder

2 tsp vanilla essence

25g (1oz) butter, melted

Add the hot water to the grated coconut and allow to stand for 30 minutes. Squeeze through muslin until you have 275ml (10fl oz) of milk.

Grate the sweet potato very finely and mix with the milk, sugar, currants, raisins and cinnamon. Add the vanilla essence and butter and mix well. Pour the mixture into a buttered ovenproof dish and bake in the oven Gas mark 4, 350°F (180°C) for about 1 hour. Serve just warm or cold with cream.

Sweet potatoes. Serves 8. Vegetarian dish.

Pone is the name given to a lightly-textured bread made from maize, which is North American in origin, but this recipe is the version used in Jamaica.

Sweet potato cake

Jamaica

450g (1 lb) sweet potatoes,
   boiled with skins on, then
   peeled
110g (4oz) icing sugar, sifted
50g (2oz) candied peel, finely
   chopped
50g (2oz) ground almonds
50g (2oz) butter, melted
2 large eggs
Sugar for dusting

Put the cooked potato through a ricer or vegetable mouli. Mix in the sugar, peel, almonds and butter. Separate the eggs and stir in the beaten yolks. Whisk whites until stiff and fold into the potato mixture. Add a little milk if too dry.

Pour into a greased 20cm (8in) sandwich tin and bake in the oven Gas mark 4, 350°F (180°C) until golden brown. Dust over with sugar and serve either hot or cold with any fruit, chocolate or butterscotch sauce.

Sweet potatoes. Serves 6.

Sweet potatoes with almonds and sherry

Bermuda

4 medium sweet potatoes
50g (2oz) butter
Pinch salt
Good grinding of black
   pepper
110g (4oz) double cream
Sherry to taste
2 tbsp toasted almonds for
   garnish

Wash and dry the potatoes and place in the oven until cooked and soft when squeezed gently, about 1 hour. Carefully take off a slice from the top of each potato and scoop out the inside, taking care not to break the skin.

Mix the scooped out flesh with all the other ingredients and fill the shells with this mixture. Bake in the oven Gas mark 8, 450°F (230°C) for 10 minutes and serve with toasted almonds sprinkled on top.

Sweet potatoes. Serves 6. Vegetarian dish.

Old fashioned sweet potato pie

U.S.A.

225g (8oz) potato shortcrust
   pastry, see page 140
175g (6oz) sweet potatoes,
   mashed
50g (2oz) sugar
25g (1oz) butter
1 medium egg, beaten
175ml (6fl oz) milk or 75ml
   (3fl oz) each of rum and
   orange
Good pinch salt

Line a 23cm (9in) flan dish with the pastry. Save the trimmings to make lattice strips for the top of the pie.

Pass the mashed sweet potatoes through a ricer or mouli. Cream the sugar and butter until light and fluffy. Now combine all the ingredients together and turn on to the pastry. Decorate in a lattice pattern with thin strips of pastry and bake in the oven Gas mark 4, 350°F (180°C) for about 30 minutes, or until the pastry is a nice golden colour.

Sweet potatoes. Serves 6.

Creole sweet potato pudding

U.S.A.

5 medium sweet potatoes,
   baked
3 medium eggs
225g (8oz) sugar
110g (4oz) butter, melted
275ml (10fl oz) milk
½ tsp salt
½ tsp black pepper

Peel potatoes and pass through a sieve. Separate the eggs and add the yolks, sugar, melted butter, milk, salt and pepper to the sieved potatoes and mix well.

Beat the egg whites until stiff but not too dry, and fold into the potato mixture. Pour into a buttered pie dish and bake in the oven Gas mark 4, 350°F (180°C) for about 1 hour until nicely browned on top. Serve with custard or whipped cream.

Sweet potatoes. Serves 6.

Sweet potato pie
U.S.A.

225g (8 oz) potato shortcrust
  pastry, see page 140
2 medium eggs
200g (8oz) sweet potato,
  mashed
100g (4oz) dark brown sugar
150ml (5fl oz) evaporated
  milk
25g (1oz) self-raising flour
1 tsp ground cinnamon
½ tsp nutmeg, grated
½ tsp ground ginger
Pinch ground cloves
½ tsp salt

Line a 23cm (9in) pie dish with potato shortcrust pastry.

Carefully blend all the filling ingredients together. Bring to a simmer over a medium heat and cook for 7 minutes until slightly thickened, stirring constantly. Pour into the pastry case and bake in the oven Gas mark 4, 350°F (180°C) for 30 minutes. Serve cold with whipped cream.

Sweet potatoes. Serves 8.

Sweet potato charlotte
New Zealand

700g (1½ lb) sweet potatoes
1 tbsp vanilla sugar
25g (1oz) plain flour
4 medium eggs, separate 2
  of the whites
175g (6oz) seedless raisins,
  soaked overnight in 2 tbsp
  dark rum
Grated rind of 1 medium
  orange
A little milk

Cook the potatoes in their skins until tender. Peel and pass through a ricer or mouli. Gradually add the sugar and flour, softening with a little milk. Beat 2 eggs plus 2 yolks and add to the potatoes, mixing thoroughly. Whisk the 2 egg whites until stiff but not too dry and fold into the potatoes with the raisins and orange rind.

Pour into a well-greased charlotte mould or a straight-sided ovenproof dish. Place this in a bain-marie, or a tin containing sufficient water to come two-thirds of the way up the mould, and bake in the oven Gas mark 4, 350°F (180°C) until set, about 35 minutes. Serve with whipped cream.

Sweet potatoes. Serves 4.

Sweet potato and walnut casserole
U.S.A.

700g (1½ lbs) sweet potato,
  mashed
2 tbsp milk
2 tbsp water
2 tbsp butter, softened
150ml (5fl oz) sour cream
1 medium egg
2 tbsp dark brown sugar
½ tsp grated ground
  cinnamon
¼ tsp grated nutmeg
2 tsp salt
A little pepper
2 tbsp walnuts, chopped

Blend together the mashed sweet potato, milk, water and butter until smooth and creamy. Stir in half the sour cream, egg, sugar and spices and pour into a greased pie dish. Bake in the oven Gas mark 4, 350°F (180°C) for 30 minutes until almost set.

Spoon the remaining sour cream over the top, sprinkle over the chopped walnuts and return to the oven to cook for a further 10 minutes. Serve hot or cold with cream.

Sweet potatoes. Serves 8.

Puddings, pies, cakes and pastries

Nowadays it is difficult to define a pudding, pastries or a cake, as so many recipes are interchangeable from one course to another. In this section of the book, a perfect example of this confusion is the recipe for chocolate profiteroles on page 116. These are a universal favourite with old and young and make a lovely addition to afternoon tea, or these small, round versions of eclairs are equally welcomed as a dessert for a formal dinner party. So many puddings, as well as cakes, can be made from short or puff pastry which includes potatoes as well as flour, see recipes on page 140. I would recommend that you try these potato-based recipes whenever you need pastry and add your own fillings and toppings.

There are many different ways to make cakes but the two methods most often used either cream the fat and sugar together before adding the dry ingredients, or mix the dry ingredients before rubbing in the fat. As potatoes contain no fat, their combination with the other ingredients in making a cake ensures lightness of texture and the addition of energy-giving carbohydrate. It is essential to sieve mashed potato or put it through a ricer when using it for cakes. Do not beat it when combining it with the other ingredients. Rather than beat, fold in carefully. Always use the type of flour recommended.

I am often asked the difference between a pie and a flan. In answer to this question, a pie is a savoury, or sweet filling, baked on a pastry-lined plate, topped with a further piece of pastry, then baked. A flan, on the other hand, is an open pastry, or sponge tart, filled with fruit or a savoury mixture. The words 'tart' and 'flan' are often used to mean the same thing, particularly in Western Europe.

Anyway, they say the proof of the pudding is in the eating, so whatever you make – enjoy!

opposite :see page 116 for Chocolate profiteroles recipe.

Chocolate profiteroles

New Zealand

(see page 114 for illustration)

50g (2oz) butter
150ml (5fl oz) water
60g (2½oz) plain flour
Pinch of salt
2 medium eggs
150g (5oz) potatoes, cooked
and sieved

To make potato choux pastry, melt the butter, add the cold water and bring to the boil. Remove from heat and, all at one time, add the flour and salt, beating continuously until the mixture is smooth and leaves the sides of the pan. Still beating, add one egg, the potato, then half of the remaining egg and beat all thoroughly, using an electric hand mixer, if available.

Pipe the choux mixture into small balls on a lightly-greased baking tray, glaze with the remaining egg and bake in the oven Gas mark 4, 350°F (180°C) for about 30 minutes, or until they feel dry. Prick each profiterole to release the air from the middle and cool on a rack. When cold, fill with whipped cream and top with chocolate icing or melted eating chocolate, or filling and topping of your choice.

Floury potatoes. Makes 6.

Potato fancies

Austria

225g (8 oz) potato choux
pastry, see page 140
25g (1oz) caster sugar
2–3 drops vanilla essence
Fat or oil for frying

175g (6oz) fresh or frozen
raspberries
50g (2oz) icing sugar, optional

Fancies: make choux pastry, adding caster sugar and vanilla essence. Heat the fat or oil until a hot and blue haze can be seen. Drop teaspoonfuls of pastry into the fat or oil and cook until puffed up and golden in colour. Drain well on absorbent paper and dredge with a little caster sugar.

Raspberry sauce: liquidise fresh or frozen raspberries with the optional addition of the icing sugar. Sieve and serve with the pastry fancies.

Floury potatoes. Makes 12.

Spiced potato cakes

Wales

450g (1 lb) potatoes, cooked
and mashed
25g (1oz) butter
25g (1oz) sugar
Pinch salt
110g (4 oz) plain flour
1 tsp baking powder
1 tsp ground cinnamon
1 medium egg

Mash the potatoes thoroughly while still warm, then add the butter and stir in the dry ingredients. Beat the egg and add to the potato mixture, blending well to make a smooth dough.

Turn the dough on to a floured surface and roll to a thickness of 2.5cm (1in). Cut into 5cm (2in) rounds, place on a greased baking tray and bake in the oven Gas mark 7, 425°F (220°C) for 20 minutes or until nicely browned. Serve hot or cold, buttered like scones.

Floury potatoes. Makes 12.

Potato chocolate cake

England

(see above)

225g (8 oz) plain chocolate

3 medium eggs

175g (6oz) sugar

225g (8 oz) butter, melted

2 tsp coffee essence

2 tbsp dark marmalade,
heated and sieved

225g (8 oz) potatoes, mashed

225g (8 oz) digestive biscuits,
finely crushed

50g (2oz) ground almonds

50g (2oz) almond flakes
toasted

Line an 18cm (7in) loose-bottomed cake tin with greased paper. Melt the chocolate in a basin over a pan of hot water. Beat the eggs and sugar until light and creamy. Fold in the melted chocolate, butter, coffee essence, marmalade, potatoes, crushed biscuits and ground almonds. When well mixed, pour into the cake tin and refrigerate for at least 4 hours. Carefully remove from the tin, discarding the greaseproof paper. Decorate by scattering the toasted almond flakes on top.

Floury potatoes. Serves 8.

Potato madeira cake
New Zealand

(see opposite)

450g (1 lb) potatoes, peeled, mashed and passed through a ricer

110g (4 oz) icing sugar, sifted

110g (4 oz) candied peel, chopped

50g (2oz) butter, melted

½ tsp vanilla essence

2 medium eggs, separated

Milk

Use this recipe for a seed cake by omitting the peel and mixing in 2 tsp caraway or cumin seeds.

Mix together the potatoes, icing sugar, peel, melted butter, vanilla and beaten egg yokes. Whisk the 2 egg whites until stiff and fold into the mixture. Add a little milk if the mixture is too stiff, then pour into a greased 20cm (8in) cake or loaf tin. Bake in the oven Gas mark 4, 350°F (180°C) for 45 minutes.

Floury potatoes. Serves 8.

Although this cake does not contain madeira, it was originally made to eat as an accompaniment to this delicious wine.

Potato cake (Kartoffeltorte)
Germany

500g (1 lb 2oz) potatoes, boiled in their jackets

7 medium egg yolks

250g (9oz) sugar

Grated peel of 2 lemons

2 tbsp semolina

2 tsp baking powder

80g (3½oz) almonds, chopped

7 medium egg whites

Juice of 2 lemons

Peel the warm potatoes and press them through a sieve or ricer. Leave to cool. Beat the egg yolks with the sugar until creamy. Add lemon peel, mashed potatoes, semolina, baking powder and almonds to the egg mixture.

Beat egg whites until stiff. Add lemon juice. Fold the egg whites into the potato mixture and when combined, put into a 27cm (10½in) round cake tin. Bake for 60 minutes at Gas mark 4, 350°F (180°C). Cool the cake and dust with icing sugar.

Floury potatoes. Serves 8.

Potato and almond cake (Kartoffeltorte)
Germany

350g (12oz) potatoes, cooked and sieved

350g (12oz) sugar

8 medium eggs, separated

110g (4 oz) ground almonds

25g (1oz) bitter almonds, finely chopped or grated

Mix all the ingredients together, except the egg whites, to form a smooth dough. An electric mixer is a great help here.

Beat the egg whites until they are stiff and appear dry. Fold into the dough, a little at a time. Place in a greased and lined 20cm (8in) cake tin and bake in the oven Gas mark 7, 425°F (220°C) for 45 minutes.

Floury potatoes. Serves 6.

Potato apple cake
Austria

225g (8 oz) self-raising flour

½ tsp powdered cinnamon

175g (6oz) butter

110g (4 oz) cooked, sieved potato

110g (4 oz) caster sugar

2 large cooking apples

2 medium eggs, beaten

Sift together the flour and cinnamon and rub in the butter. Add the sugar, potato and finely sliced apple. Stir in the beaten eggs to make a fairly soft consistency using a little milk if necessary.

Place the mixture in a well-greased 20cm (8in) cake tin and bake at Gas mark 5, 375°F (190°C) for 1¼ hours. Allow to cool slightly in the tin, remove and dredge with icing sugar.

Floury potatoes. Serves 8.

Orange sandwich cake *Austria*

110g (4oz) soft margarine
110g (4oz) soft brown sugar
2 oranges, juice and rind
50g (2oz) carrot, grated
2 medium eggs, beaten
175g (6oz) potatoes, cooked
  and sieved
225g (8oz) self raising flour
2 tsp baking powder
1 tsp cinnamon
1 tsp ground ginger
50g (2oz) sultanas
275ml (10fl oz) double cream
1 tbsp icing sugar, sieved

Cream together the margarine, sugar and the grated rind of the two oranges. Stir in the grated carrot and gradually add the beaten eggs. Fold in the sieved potatoes, flour, baking powder, cinnamon, ginger and sultanas. Mix in 4 tbsp of the orange juice to give a soft consistency.

Divide the mixture between 2 greased and lined 20cm (8in) sandwich tins and bake for 30 minutes at Gas mark 3, 325°F (160°C). When the cakes have cooled, sandwich together with the double cream, whipped with a little more of the orange rind. Dust with the icing sugar.

Floury potatoes. Serves 8.

Almond tart *Portugal*
(see opposite)

175g (6oz) shortcrust potato
  pastry, see page 140
3 tbsp sieved raspberry jam
1 tbsp lemon juice
75g (3oz) butter
75g (3oz) sugar
150g (5oz) potatoes, cooked
2 medium eggs, beaten
50g (2oz) ground almonds

Grease a 20cm (8in) flan dish and line with the potato pastry saving the trimmings. Spread the jam evenly over the pastry and sprinkle the lemon juice over the jam.

Cream the butter and sugar until light and fluffy. Pass the cooked potato through a sieve or ricer. Combine the butter, sugar, eggs, potatoes, and ground almonds and mix thoroughly. Turn into potato case and use the trimmings of pastry to make a lattice pattern on top.

Bake in the oven Gas mark 7, 425°F (220°C) for 15 minutes. Reduce heat to Gas mark 4, 350°F (180°C) and bake until the filling is firm, about 25 minutes. Serve hot or cold.

Floury potatoes. Serves 6.

Rhubarb and potato cobbler *England*

450g (1 lb) rhubarb
110g (4oz) sugar, or to taste

110g (4oz) butter
225g (8oz) self-raising flour,
  sifted
50g (2oz) caster sugar
Pinch salt
225g (8oz) cooked, sieved
  potatoes

Filling: wash and trim the rhubarb and cut into pieces. Put the rhubarb into a greased pie dish with sufficient sugar to sweeten. Place in the oven to cook, Gas mark 6, 400°F (200°C) while you make the topping.

Topping: rub the butter into the sifted flour, add caster sugar and salt. Stir in the potato and knead all together to form a scone-type dough. Roll out on a lightly floured surface to about 1cm (½in) thick, cut into rounds and cover the hot fruit with the dough rounds.

Replace in the oven and bake for about 15 minutes, until the cobbler is well-risen and golden brown. Dredge with sifted icing sugar and serve hot.

Floury potatoes. Serves 8. Vegetarian dish.

Steamed rich pudding *Scotland*

(see opposite)

175g (6oz) grated raw potato
175g (6oz) grated raw carrot
175g (6oz) caster sugar
110g (4oz) shredded suet
110g (4oz) self-raising flour
3 medium eggs, beaten
¾ tsp grated nutmeg

Mix all ingredients thoroughly, put into a lightly-greased 1.15 lt (2 pt) basin, cover and steam for 2½–3 hours, taking care to top up the steamer with boiling water when necessary.

Floury potatoes. Serves 6.

Steamed fruit pudding *Scotland*

225g (8 oz) self-raising flour
110g (4 oz) cooked, sieved potatoes
110g (4 oz) shredded suet
Pinch salt
Cold water to mix

3 large cooking apples
75g (3oz) sultanas
110g (4oz) soft brown sugar

Pudding: sift flour and salt lightly, mix in the potato and suet. Add sufficient water to bind into a soft dough. Take two-thirds of the dough and use to line a well-greased 1.15 lt (2 pt) pudding basin.

Filling: fill with layers of sliced apple, then a sprinkling of sultanas and sugar. Pour over 2 tbsp cold water, cover with remaining dough, pressing the edges firmly together to seal. Cover with a lid of greaseproof paper tied firmly in place with string and steam for 2 hours. Do not allow to boil dry, but add boiling water when required.

Floury potatoes. Serves 6.

Steamed chocolate pudding *England*

175g (6oz) butter
200g (7oz) caster sugar
2 medium eggs
225g (8 oz) self-raising flour, sifted
50g (2oz) cocoa powder
175g (6oz) cooked, sieved potatoes
3–4 tbsp milk
Pinch salt

Cream the butter and caster sugar till light and fluffy. Beat the eggs thoroughly and add to the butter mixture. Stir in the sifted flour, cocoa powder, potato and salt. Add sufficient milk to make a soft consistency.

Pour the chocolate mixture into a greased 1.15 lt (2 pt) basin, cover and steam for 1½ hours. Turn out and serve with either custard or a chocolate sauce.

Floury potatoes. Serves 6.

Steamed date pudding *England*

225g (8 oz) cooked, sieved potatoes
75g (3oz) chopped, stoned dates
1 medium egg, beaten
25g (1oz) caster sugar
50g (2oz) melted butter
1 orange, rind grated, plus juice
Pinch salt

Mix all ingredients thoroughly, adding sufficient orange juice to make a soft consistency. Put pudding mixture into a lightly-greased 900ml (1½ pt) basin, cover and steam for 1½ hours, adding boiling water to the pan of the steamer when necessary.

Floury potatoes. Serves 4.

Potato, syrup and chocolate pudding   *Holland*

110g (4 oz) butter, melted
450g (1 lb) potatoes, cooked and sieved
1 medium egg, beaten
1 lemon, juice and grated rind
2 tbsp golden syrup
25g (1oz) self-raising flour
1 tsp baking powder

2 tbsp golden syrup
2 tbsp cocoa powder
2 tbsp warm water

Pudding: beat together the melted butter and potatoes. Add the beaten egg, lemon juice and rind, the syrup, flour and baking powder. Bake in a well-buttered charlotte mould about 18cm (7in) diameter, in the oven Gas mark 5, 375°F (190°C) for 1 hour.

Sauce: mix together the syrup, cocoa powder and warm water. Heat until ingredients are completely dissolved.

Pour this over the pudding, turn the oven temperature up to Gas mark 6, 440°F (200°C) and bake for a further 15 minutes.

Floury potatoes. Serves 6.

Potato and summer fruit pudding   *Denmark*

700g (1½ lb) redcurrants
700g (1½ lb) raspberries
175g (6oz) sugar
Vanilla essence, few drops
175g (6oz) potato flour
25g (1oz) caster sugar
275ml (10fl oz) whipped cream
110g (4 oz) almonds or walnuts, chopped

Wash and drain the redcurrants and raspberries and cook gently to let the juices run. Add the sugar and vanilla essence. Continue cooking until most of the liquid has evaporated. Thicken with potato flour but do not allow to boil, just to cook through.

Serve well chilled, having sprinkled the caster sugar over the top to prevent a skin forming, and decorate with the whipped cream and chopped nuts.

Potato flour. Serves 8. Vegetarian dish.

Potato flour is ideal for thickening sauces and soups and is available from health food shops.

Pineapple upside down pudding   *Canada*

2 tbsp golden syrup, warmed
220g (7¾oz) can pineapple slices and juice
4 glacé cherries, halved
175g (6oz) soft margarine
175g (6oz) caster sugar
110g (4oz) potatoes, cooked and sieved
2 medium eggs, beaten
175g (6oz) self-raising flour
Fresh cream

Thoroughly grease a 18cm (7in) round tin. Pour the golden syrup into the base of this and arrange the pineapple slices and cherries on top of the syrup.

Beat the margarine, sugar and potatoes until light and fluffy and gradually stir in the beaten eggs. Fold in the flour. Stir in the pineapple juice until a soft consistency is reached. Pour the mixture over the pineapple, smooth the top and bake in the oven Gas mark 4, 350°F (180°C) for about 65 minutes. Turn out on to a flat plate with the pineapple side at the top and serve with fresh cream.

Floury potatoes. Serves 8.

Peach, potato and meringue pie

110g (4 oz) shortcrust potato
pastry, see page 140

225g (8 oz) cooked, sliced
peaches

50g (2oz) butter

50g (2oz) caster sugar

2 medium egg yolks

Almond essence

50g (2oz) self-raising flour,
sifted

110g (4 oz) cooked, sieved
potato

Pinch salt

A little peach juice

Pie: line a flan ring or deep pie plate with the pastry and arrange the sliced peaches evenly over the bottom. Beat together the butter, sugar, egg yolks and essence. Fold in the sifted flour, potato and salt and add sufficient juice to make a soft consistency. Pour this mixture evenly over the peaches and bake in the oven Gas mark 5, 375°F (190°C) for 30 minutes.

2 egg whites

110g (4 oz) caster sugar

Meringue: whisk the egg whites stiffly, whisk in half the sugar and fold in the remainder. Cover the flan with the meringue and brown in the oven Gas mark 5, 375°F (190°C) for 10 minutes. Serve hot or cold.

Floury potatoes. Serves 6.

Tinned peaches can be used for this recipe but drain off the syrup or fruit juice before use.

Onslow pie

175g (6oz) shortcrust potato
pastry, see page 140

175g (6oz) cooked, sieved
potatoes

50g (2oz) butter, melted

50g (2oz) caster sugar

50g (2oz) sultanas

2 medium eggs, separated

Line a pie plate with half the pastry. Mix together the potatoes, butter, sugar, sultanas and egg yolks. Whip the egg whites until stiff and carefully fold into the potato mixture.

Fill the pastry case, cover with the remaining pastry, brush the top with egg yolk or milk and sprinkle well with sugar. Bake in the oven at Gas mark 6, 400°F (200°C) for 30 minutes.

Floury potatoes. Serves 6.

Breads, scones and pancakes

When making potato dough, the same basic principles apply as when making ordinary breads, that is, kneading, rising, knocking back and, finally, baking. Adding potato to the dough gives it a lovely, soft, moist consistency, which also means it will keep fresh for a longer period.

Use a strong white flour combined with potato, as it is higher in gluten-forming proteins and gives the bread its structure. Kneading helps to distribute the gluten and this is better achieved by using the 'heels' of your hands. Push down on the dough and away from you, then fold in half towards you, quarter turn, and repeat several times until you have a nice elastic consistency.

All yeast mixtures should be allowed to rise at least once, as this gives the yeast a chance to work. Dough should be allowed to double in size and it is important to make sure that it is left in an even, warm temperature, but not above 90°F (32°C) for about one hour. Normal room temperature will take about 2 hours.

The process known as 'knocking back' or 'kneading" can now take place before shaping the dough. This procedure consists of breaking up the dough once it has become elastic by working it with the heel of the hand. It knocks out the air bubbles and ensures that the dough rises evenly and has a good texture. Baking should take place in a fairly high temperature to kill off the yeast. To tell if the dough is cooked, tap the base of the bread and if it sounds hollow, it is ready.

The scone recipes in this chapter are for both savoury and sweet versions, although the Scottish potato scone can be either; sweet if spread with butter and jam while still hot, or savoury when fried with bacon for breakfast.

Recipes for potato pancakes vary not just from country to country but from British county to county. Whatever the method of baking or cooking, they are delicious as part of a hearty breakfast, or as a base for a teatime snack.

Opposite: see page 133 for Potato scones recipe.

Potato bread (Potato puri) *India*

225g (8 oz) potatoes, cooked
225g (8 oz) plain flour, sieved
2 tsp salt
Warm water to bind
Sufficient oil for deep-frying

Mash the cooked potatoes or rub through a sieve. Knead for 3 to 4 minutes. Knead the flour and salt into the potatoes, and gradually add sufficient warm water to make a stiff pastry. Knead again, then divide the mixture into 12 pieces and roll each piece into a circular shape, but not too thin.

Heat the oil in a deep pan and fry each potato circle separately, spooning the oil over the top to make them rise and cook to a golden brown. Drain and serve hot or cold.

Floury potatoes. Makes 12. Vegetarian dish.

Potato flatbread *Norway*

900g (2 lb) potatoes, peeled
1 tsp salt
2 tbsp butter
225g (8 oz) self-raising flour

Preheat a griddle or strong frying pan till fairly hot.

Cut up the potatoes and cook until tender but not mushy, about 20 minutes. Drain and dry off slightly. Pass potatoes through a ricer or sieve, then add the salt and butter. Cool until just warm.

Stir in 175g (6oz) of the flour, then enough of the remaining 50g (2oz) to make a stiff dough. Divide into four portions, then each portion into 4 equal pieces. On a lightly floured board roll out 1 piece of dough at a time to a paper-thin circle. Bake each dough circle on the pre-heated griddle for 1 to 2 minutes on each side, until browned in spots. The resulting bread will look dry but will be flexible, not crisp. Fold in half, then in half again and stack on waxed paper as they are baked. To serve, unfold and spread with butter.

Floury potatoes. Makes 16. Vegetarian dish.

This bread is used by Norwegians for all special occasions and is very similar to Scottish potato scones. Norwegians use a special rolling pin called a 'lefse' which gives a grid-like texture. This recipe will freeze well.

Boxty bread *Ireland*
(see opposite)

450g (1 lb) raw potatoes, grated
450g (1 lb) potatoes, cooked and mashed
350g (12oz) plain flour
10g (½oz) baking powder
1 tsp salt
110g (4 oz) butter, softened but not melted

Put the grated potatoes into a clean piece of muslin and squeeze out as much moisture as possible. Now combine the raw potato, mashed potato, flour, baking powder, salt and butter.

Turn the mixture on to a well-floured surface and divide into four equal portions. Roll each into a round about 6mm (¼in) thick and mark into four quarters. Place on a greased baking tray and bake in the oven Gas mark 4, 350°F (180°C) for 40 minutes. Divide into four and serve very hot with butter.

Floury potatoes. Makes 16. Vegetarian dish.

A favourite traditional bread, originally created to save the precious wheat flour, which was more expensive than potatoes.

White potato bread

5g (¼oz) active dried yeast
75ml (3fl oz) warm potato
water
25g (1oz) sugar
50g (2oz) butter, slightly
softened
3 medium eggs
2 tsp salt
175g (6oz) cooked and
mashed potatoes
150ml (5fl oz) boiled and
cooled milk
700g (1½ lb) bread, or self-
raising flour

Lightly grease two 23cm × 13cm (9in × 5in) loaf tins. In a large bowl stir the yeast into the warm water at a temperature of about 110°F (45°C) and leave to soften and froth. Stirring constantly, add the sugar, butter, eggs, salt, potatoes and milk, then beat all to a smooth batter. Add the flour a little at a time to make a stiff dough. Turn on to a lightly floured board, cover with a tea cloth and leave to rise for 10 minutes.

Remove the tea cloth and knead the dough until smooth for about eight minutes, and return to the large bowl, cover and leave to rise in a warm place until it has doubled in size, about 2 hours. Knead the dough with your knuckles, then divide into equal parts and shape into the loaf tins and again leave to rise for a further 60 minutes.

Bake in the oven Gas mark 5, 375°F (190°C) until golden brown and the loaves sound hollow when tapped with your fingers. Turn out of the tins and cool on the rack.

Floury potatoes. Makes 2 loaves.

This is another recipe for using leftover potatoes. Sometimes I cook extra for the sole purpose of making this bread.

Potato bread rolls

75g (3oz) packet instant
potato mix
275ml (10fl oz) boiling water
275ml (10fl oz) milk
110g (4 oz) margarine or
butter
50g (2oz) sugar
1 tsp salt
2 tsp dried yeast
110ml (4fl oz) lukewarm
water
2 medium eggs, beaten
735g (1 lb 10oz) strong plain
flour, sieved

Make up the potato mix with the boiling water. Mix in the milk, margarine or butter, sugar and salt. Stir to melt the margarine, then allow to cool until lukewarm. Dissolve the yeast in the lukewarm water and add to the mixture with the eggs. Add 175g (6oz) of flour and beat until smooth. Cover and stand in a warm place for about 2 hours, until full of bubbles.

Add sufficient of the remaining flour to make a soft dough. Turn out and knead for 5 minutes. Cover with greased polythene and allow to rise until double in bulk then knead again for 1 minute. Divide into two equal portions. Shape each portion into a roll and cut into 16 pieces. Roll each piece into a long sausage shape and twist lightly. Lay on greased baking trays, cover with greased polythene and allow to rise again until double in size.

Brush with a little salt dissolved in hot water. Bake in the oven Gas mark 7, 425°F (220°C) for 10–12 minutes.

Instant potato mix. Makes 16.

Potato rolls   *Wales*

450g (1 lb) plain flour
110g (4 oz) potatoes, freshly
    boiled and mashed
25g (1oz) yeast
50g (2oz) sugar
150ml (5fl oz) warm milk
150ml (5fl oz) water
1 tsp salt
50g (2oz) butter
1 medium egg, beaten
Milk to glaze

Sieve and warm the flour. Put the mashed potatoes through a sieve and keep warm. Mix the yeast with 25g (1oz) sugar and a little of the warm milk. Rub the salt and butter into the flour. Add the remaining sugar and mashed potatoes. Add a little more milk to the yeast together with the beaten egg and stir into the flour and potatoes with the water to make a soft dough. Knead thoroughly, cover and leave to rise until double in size.

Turn out on to a well-floured surface. Cut up and shape into rolls. Put on a greased baking sheet and prove for 10 to 15 minutes. Brush with a little milk and bake in the oven Gas mark 6, 400°F (200°C) for 15 minutes.

Floury potatoes. Makes 16.

Potato pooris   *India*

1 medium sized potato,
    freshly cooked in its jacket
150g (5oz) plain white flour
½ tsp salt
½ tsp ground cumin seeds
½ tsp garam masala,
see page 26
1 tbsp fresh coriander,
    chopped
1½ tbsp vegetable oil
Sufficient vegetable oil for
    frying

Peel the potato while still hot and mash thoroughly, putting through a ricer if possible. Allow to cool slightly.

Sieve the flour, salt, cumin, garam masala and coriander into a bowl. Add the mashed potato and with the fingertips combine with the flour mixture. Add the oil and rub in well to form a dough. A little water may be needed to bind the mixture and the dough should be very firm. Knead the dough for 10 minutes and form into a ball, coat with oil and place in a plastic bag and leave to rest for 20 minutes. Knead the dough again for a few minutes then divide into 8 equal parts and cover with cling film.

Heat the oil in a deep frying pan or wok, noting that a depth of 6cm (2¼in) of oil is required, and wait until the oil becomes very hot. While the oil is heating, form each of the 8 pieces of dough into balls. Taking one at a time, flatten the ball in the palm of your hand and put on a lightly floured surface, and roll out evenly with a rolling pin to a round of 15cm (6in) diameter. Fry each poori in the hot oil by laying it carefully on top of the oil, when it should start to sizzle. Gently push the poori under the oil with the back of a draining spoon. In a very short time it should balloon. Turn it over and cook on the underside for a few seconds. Remove and drain on absorbent kitchen paper, which is lining a large bowl. Cover the bowl with a lid or plate to keep the poori warm while you cook the rest.

Floury potatoes. Makes 8. Vegetarian dish.

White flour and mashed potatoes are used in making this popular recipe for fried potato bread. They are best eaten as soon as they are made. If you keep them to eat later they will have deflated, but will still taste delicious.

Savoury herb scones

Canada

(see above)

110g (4oz) potatoes, cooked
and sieved

110g (4oz) self raising flour

75g (3oz) lard, or any fat

Good pinch of salt

Good pinch of cayenne
pepper

2 tbsp mixed parsley and
chives, chopped

1 medium egg, beaten with
sufficient milk to make a
soft dough

50g (2oz) cornflakes, crushed

Mix together the sieved potato and flour. Rub in the fat and add the salt, cayenne pepper and herbs. Mix to a soft dough with the egg and milk, but save a little to brush over the top of the scones.

Roll out the dough to a 1cm (½in) thick oblong shape. Sprinkle the crushed cornflakes over the top. Roll the dough up like a large sausage, cut into even slices, flatten slightly with your hand, brush over with a little of the beaten egg and milk. Bake in a hot oven Gas mark 6, 400°F (200°C) for 15 minutes or until nicely risen and golden in colour.

Floury potatoes. Makes 8 scones.

Potato scones

Scotland

(see page 127 for illustration)

75g (3oz) plain flour
Good pinch salt
450g (1 lb) mashed potatoes, cold
Milk to mix to a firm dough

Heat a griddle or thick frying pan until quite hot. Meanwhile, sift the flour and salt and knead into the cold potato, adding sufficient milk to make a fairly stiff dough. The type of potato used will determine the amount of milk.

Divide the dough into four equal portions. Taking one portion at a time, roll out to a circle about 6mm (¼in) thick. Cut each circle into four wedge shapes and bake on the griddle, without using any fat, until nicely browned on both sides.

Allow to cool wrapped in a clean tea towel that has been placed on a cooling rack.

Floury potatoes. Makes 16. Vegetarian dish.

As a child, I well remember pressing my nose against the shop window of Ross's Dairies to watch them make these scones. They can be served warm with lashings of butter for tea, but the favourite way to eat them in my family is to fry them until crisp in bacon fat and serve them with bacon and eggs, plus trimmings, for breakfast.

Pratie cakes

Ireland

450g (1 lb) potatoes
1 tsp salt
25g (1oz) plain flour

Heat a griddle so that it is fairly hot and grease.

Cook the potatoes in boiling salted water until tender, drain and allow to dry off. Put through a ricer or sieve on to a well-floured surface. Sprinkle the flour over and carefully knead into the potato to make a light dough.

Roll out to a thickness of 6mm (¼in) and cut into rounds with a 5cm (2in) scone cutter. Bake on the griddle until a deep golden brown on both sides. Butter and serve at once.

Floury potatoes. Makes 14. Vegetarian dish.

Potato fruit scones

Switzerland

110g (4 oz) butter
225g (8 oz) self-raising flour
175g (6oz) cooked, sieved potatoes
Pinch salt
50g (2oz) caster sugar
Milk to mix

110g (4 oz) mixed, dried fruit
110g (4 oz) soft brown sugar
½ tsp mixed spice

Scones: rub butter into flour, salt and potatoes. Add the sugar and sufficient milk to bind to a soft dough. Roll out on a lightly floured surface to make a rectangle about 6mm (¼in) thick. Brush over with a little milk.

Filling: mix the ingredients and cover the scone dough. Roll up the dough, sealing the edges, and slice into about 12 pieces. Place these, cut side down, on to a well-greased baking sheet and bake in the oven Gas mark 8, 450°F (230°C) for about 10 minutes.

Floury potatoes. Makes 12. Vegetarian dish.

Potato pancakes (Kartoffelpfannkuchen) *Germany*

(see opposite)

1kg (2.2lb) potatoes
1 tsp salt
1 onion, chopped
1 medium egg
25g (1oz) flour
Fat to fry

I prefer to use beef dripping or bacon fat.

2 large cooking apples
25g (1oz) butter
2 tbsp water
50g (2oz) sugar
½ tsp cinnamon

Pancakes: peel the potatoes and grate them on the fine side of the grater. Add the salt, onion, egg and flour. Mix well. Heat the fat until it smokes. Shape the mixture into thin, flat pancakes, and fry them quickly on both sides.

Sauce: peel, core and slice the apples and cook gently with the butter, water, sugar and cinnamon. When soft and pulpy, beat thoroughly and rub through a sieve, or liquidise. Divide the sauce between the eight pancakes and serve.

Floury potatoes. Makes 8.

This delicious dish used to be served to the shift workers from stalls in Köln at four in the morning. Alas, no more! In Palatinat, they are eaten with lots of apple sauce and are considered a main meal.

Potato pancakes with bacon and banana *South Africa*

175g (6oz) potatoes, mashed
75g (3oz) plain flour
1 medium egg
275ml (10fl oz) milk
Salt and pepper to taste
25g (1oz) butter
2 large bananas
4 bacon rashers, cut into strips

Mix together the mashed potatoes and flour. Make a well in the centre and drop in the egg. Gradually stir in the milk to make a batter. Season with salt and pepper to taste. Heat the butter and cook the batter to make 4 pancakes, then keep warm.

Peel and quarter the bananas. Fry the bacon until crisp and pour off any excess fat from the pan but leave sufficient to gently fry the banana pieces. Divide the fried bananas between the four pancakes and roll each pancake up. Top with the crisp bacon strips and serve.

Floury potatoes. Serves 4.

My good friend Meg lived in South Africa for many years and gave me this recipe. She also has a great penchant for bacon and banana sandwiches!

Grated potato pancakes *Holland*

900g (2 lb) potatoes
1 small onion
2 medium eggs, beaten
3 tbsp flour
¼ tsp ground nutmeg
¼ tsp ground pepper
1 tsp salt
½ tsp baking powder
Butter or margarine for cooking
Parsley for garnish

Peel and finely grate the raw potatoes and onion into a bowl and leave to stand for 10 minutes. Drain off any liquid which collects in the bowl. Add the eggs and all the other ingredients, except the butter and parsley, to the bowl and beat well until smooth.

Melt the butter in a heavy frying pan and, when hot, drop spoonfuls of the batter into the hot butter and cook for about 3 minutes. Turn the pancakes and cook on the other side for a further 2–3 minutes until golden brown. Drain well on kitchen paper. Serve garnished with parsley.

Waxy or floury potatoes. Makes 20.

Wine

The making of wine was probably discovered entirely by accident, when the delicious flavour and intoxicating effects of drinking fruit juices, which had been fermented from natural yeasts, proved so enjoyable! Wine was almost an everyday beverage in the ancient Mediterranean countries and it was certainly a commonplace commodity in Egypt, Greece and Italy long before the birth of Christ. There are many references in the Bible to vineyards, grapes and wine itself, and it is widely believed that Noah was the first viniculturist. Although the potato originated in South America, it does not appear to have been used as the basis of an alcoholic beverage, the natives preferring beer made from maize and manioc.

Since its discovery, the potato has been fermented with the addition of other ingredients, and the wine distilled into spirit in almost every country. In Ethiopia it is fermented with honey; in Canada with hops and ginger; Germany and Norway steam the potatoes in vats then mix with malt to make a type of beer; the French and Hungarians harvest the berry that forms after flowering and make a version of brandy and the Irish make a kind of poteen, authentic poteen being made from barley distilled over a peat fire in the open air. In the days of prohibition in America, many dubious ingredients, including potatoes, were used to make 'hooch'. This term is derived from the North American Indian word, 'hootchino.'

The following guidelines will help you to achieve the best results. You will need a suitable large container for boiling, but not made from iron, brass or copper; a large plastic bin for brewing; a plastic bucket; wine bottles and a wooden spoon. Always use clean utensils; try different wine yeasts for varying results; always use new corks; keep one bottle beyond its recommended drinking time to test its lifetime; do not allow fermenting wine to come into contact with metal; do not bottle wine too early, especially if it is still fermenting; remove all pith from citrus fruits before use.

For all the recipes in this section use waxy or floury potatoes.

Opposite: some ingredients and equipment used in making potato wines

Potato and ginger wine

Canada

2.25 kg (5 lb) potatoes
4.5 lt (1 gallon) water
2 lemons
1 orange
25g (1oz) root ginger, well
  chopped
2 kg (4 lb 6oz) demerara sugar
25g (1oz) bakers' yeast

Scrub the potatoes but do not peel. Cut into quarters and boil in water for 20 minutes. Strain the water off and retain. Discard the potatoes.

Peel the lemons and orange and finely shred the skins, removing as much pith as possible. Pour the hot potato water over the skins and add the chopped ginger; make the liquid up to 4.5 lt (1 gallon), and bring to the boil. Allow to simmer for 15 minutes. Add the sugar and fruit juices and the yeast, which has previously been mixed with a little warm water. Stir well.

Cover and leave for 24 hours in a warm place. Strain and put into a fermenting jar and insert an airlock, then leave to finish fermenting in a warm place. When fermentation has ceased, syphon off and bottle. Allow to stand for at least 3 months. Makes 4.5 lt (1 gallon).

Potato and hop wine

England

1.8 kg (4 lb) potatoes
1 lemon
1 handful of hops
4.5 lt (1 gallon) water
1.6 kg (3 lb 8oz) demerara
  sugar
50g (2oz) yeast and yeast
  nutrient

Boil the potatoes in the water until just tender, but not broken, together with the lemon and the hops. Strain and pour potato liquid over the sugar. Stir well.

When cooled to 68°F (20°C), add the yeast and yeast nutrient. Leave in a warm place for 24 hours. Put the liquid into a barrel and cork loosely. When fermentation has ceased, cork tightly and leave for 3 weeks. Syphon off and bottle. Allow to stand for 3 months. Makes 4.5 lt (1 gallon).

Potato, ginger and fruit wine

Canada

2.25 kg (5 lb) potatoes
4.5 lt (1 gallon) water
2 lemons, peeled
1 orange, peeled
150g (5oz) root ginger, well
  bruised
1.6 kg (3 lb 8oz) demerara
  sugar
20g (¾oz) yeast and yeast
  nutrient

Boil the potatoes in the water until just tender, but not broken. Strain and discard potatoes. Add the liquid to the peel from the lemons and orange, and the ginger. Boil for 10 minutes. Add the sugar and stir well. Allow to cool.

When cooled to 68°F (20°C), add the juices of the lemons and the orange and the yeast and yeast nutrient. Cover and leave for 24 hours. Strain into a jar to ferment. When fermentation has ceased, syphon off and bottle. Allow to stand for 3 months. Makes 4.5 lt (1 gallon).

Potato and barley wine

Scotland

1 lemon
1 orange
1 large potato
450g (1 lb) pearl barley
450g (1 lb) raisins
2 kg (4 lb 6oz) demerara sugar
4.5 lt (1 gallon) boiling water
25g (1oz) bakers' yeast

Peel and finely shred the lemon and orange skins, removing as much pith as possible, and put into a large bowl together with the juices. Scrub but do not peel the potato. Slice and add to the bowl, then add the barley, raisins and sugar. Pour the boiling water over all and stir well.

When cooled to lukewarm, add the yeast previously creamed with a little of the warm liquid. Cover and leave to ferment in a warm place for three to four weeks. Stir daily. When fermentation has ceased, syphon off and bottle. Allow to stand for 3 months. Makes 4.5 lt (1 gallon).

Potato and raisin wine

Germany

2 large potatoes, peeled and sliced
900g (2 lb) raisins
225g (8 oz) wheat
1 lemon, sliced
2 kg (4 lb 6oz) demerara sugar
4.5 lt (1 gallon) water, hot
25g (1oz) yeast, creamed with a little water

Put all the ingredients, except the yeast, into an earthenware bowl and pour over the water which should be hot but not boiling. When cool, add the creamed yeast.

Cover and leave standing in a warm place for 21 days. Stir daily. Strain and bottle but leave for a further week before inserting the corks. Allow to stand for 3 months. Makes 4.5 lt (1 gallon).

Potato and onion wine

Norway

225g (8 oz) onions, peeled and diced
225g (8 oz) potatoes, peeled and diced
450g (1 lb) raisins, chopped
1 kg 350g (3 lb) white sugar
4.5 lt (1 gallon) water, warm
2 tsp citric acid
1 tsp yeast nutrient
25g (1oz) bakers' yeast

Put the diced onions and potatoes together with the chopped raisins into an earthenware bowl and pour over the warm water, not hot, which has had the sugar dissolved in it. Add the citric acid and yeast nutrient. Soften the yeast with a little of the warm water and, when foaming, add to the rest of the ingredients.

Cover and leave for 15 days. Strain into glass jars and fit fermentation locks. When fermentation has ceased, bottle and cork. Allow to stand for 6 months. Makes 4.5 lt (1 gallon).

Potato hock

Germany

25g (1oz) yeast
4.5 lt (1 gallon) water, hot
2 oranges
2 lemons
450g (1 lb) raisins
6 medium potatoes, scrubbed and sliced
2 kg (4 lb 6oz) white sugar

Cream the yeast with a little of the water which should be hot but not boiling, and leave to froth.

Peel the oranges and lemons and finely shred the skins, removing as much pith as possible. Squeeze the juice of the oranges and lemons. Chop the raisins as finely as possible. Put all the ingredients into a suitable container and pour over the hot water.

Cover and allow to stand for about 2 weeks. Stir daily. When fermentation has ceased, syphon off and bottle. Allow to stand for 3 months. Makes 4.5 lt (1 gallon).

Basic recipes

Potato stock   *England*

2 large potatoes
3 large carrots
2 onions
3 stalks celery
1.145 lt (2 pt) cold water
Salt and pepper to taste
Bunch of mixed herbs

Wash but do not peel the potatoes and carrots; roughly chop. Peel and roughly chop the onions. De-string and chop the celery, using tops also. Place in a suitable pan and pour over the water. Season with salt and pepper and add the mixed herbs.

Bring to the boil gently and allow to simmer until the vegetables are well cooked. Depending on how you wish to use the stock, either clear or opaque, strain off the liquid, or rub the ingredients through a sieve and add to the liquid.

Floury potatoes. Makes 900ml (1½pt).

A good stock forms the basis of all successful soup recipes. If you freeze this stock it can be used when required.

Potato shortcrust pastry   *Scotland*

110g (4 oz) self-raising flour
50g (2oz) potatoes, peeled,
    cooked and riced
1 level tsp salt
75g (3oz) butter
Cold water to bind

Mix all dry ingredients together and rub in the butter. Add sufficient water to bind, cover with cling-film and allow to stand for at least 45 minutes. Roll out and use for all pies, flans and quiches.

Floury potatoes. Makes sufficient for a 20.5cm (8in) dish.

Potato puff pastry   *England*

150g (5oz) self-raising flour
75g (3oz) potatoes, peeled,
    cooked and riced
1 level tsp salt
110g (4 oz) butter
75ml (3fl oz) water, very cold
50g (2oz) butter

Mix all dry ingredients together and rub in the 110g (4 oz) butter. Bind with the water. Cover and allow to rest for 10 minutes.

Roll out to an oblong shape, dot some of the 50g (2oz) butter over two-thirds of the pastry and fold in three. Seal the edges, turn the pastry round and roll out to an oblong and repeat the butter and folding routine three times. Leave covered for at least 2 hours in the refrigerator before use.

Floury potatoes. Makes sufficient for a 20.5cm (8in) dish.

Choux pastry   *France*

60g (2½oz) plain flour
50g (2oz) butter
150ml (5fl oz) water
Pinch of salt
2 medium eggs, beaten
150g (5oz) potatoes, cooked
    and sieved

Pass the flour twice through a fine sieve. Melt the butter in the water over a low heat and when melted, bring to a fast boil. Remove from heat and, all at one time, add the flour and the salt, beating continuously until the mixture is smooth and leaves the sides of the pan to form a soft ball.

Still beating, add the eggs a little at a time alternately with the sieved potato, (an electric hand mixer is excellent for this job). The finished pastry should be firm but soft.

Floury potatoes. Makes sufficient for a 20.5cm (8in) dish.

Vegetarian dishes

Indexes

GENERAL INDEX

Abbreviations 13
Baked potatoes 100–107
Fillings
  Bacon and sweetcorn 107
  Beef and mushroom with horseradish 106
  Cream cheese and spring onion 103
  Hot dog and sweetcorn 106
  Lemon and chutney 103
  Liver mushroom and onion 106
  Pineapple yogurt and cheese 104
  Savoury minced beef and tomato 107
  Sour cream and Parmesan 103
  Tuna and potato 105
Sauces
  Horseradish 102
  Sour cream 102
  Tangy orange 103
Toppings
  Boozy prawn and pepper 104
  Smoked ham and pineapple 106
  Turkey and broccoli 105
  Turkey and ham 105
Potato Chantilly 102
Basic recipes
Choux pastry 140
Puff pastry 140
Shortcrust pastry 140
Stock 140
Breads, scones and pancakes 126–135
  Boxty 128
  Flatbread, potato 128
  Potato 128
  White potato 130
Cakes, pratie 133
Pancakes
  Grated potato 135
  Potato 135
  Potato with bacon and banana 135
Pooris, potato 131
Rolls 131
  Potato 131
  Potato bread 130
Scones
  Potato 133
  Potato fruit 133
  Savoury herb 132
Cakes, see 'Puddings, pies, cakes and pastries'
Classics and side dishes 48–63
Croquettes
  Potato 57
  Milanese 60
Balls
  Cheesy potato 58
  Potato 58
  Turkish potato 58
Champ 62
Chips 50
Croutons, potato 51
Potatoes, creamy fried 62
Potato à la maître d'hôtel 55
Potato and onion medley 61
Potato borders 57

Potatoes
  à l'hongroise 60
  à la landaise 59
  à la paysanne 55
  with garlic and sesame 53
  with whole spices and sesame 53
  Anna 52
  Byron 59
  Caramelized 55
  Château 49, 55
  Châtouillard 52
  Crainquebille 62
  Crunchy roast 56
  Darfin 52
  Dauphin 63
  Duchess 49, 57
  Hasselback 54
  Herbed 53
  Lorette 56
  Lyonnaise 61
  Parmentier 51
  Puréed 63
  Sauté 50
  Soufflé 50
Quenelles, potato with Parmesan 60
Rissole potatoes 52
Rosti 56
Garam masala 26
Hors d'oeuvres and salads 16–35
Apples, potato stuffed 27
Chutney, potato 21
Crisps, potato 19
Dressings
  Bumbu 26
  Peanut and chilli 28
  Potato for potato salad 21
  Wine 21
Fritters, potato 19
Mayonnaise, potato and egg 19
Mussels with potatoes 33
Potato slices with caviar 20
Salads
  Bean curd and cooked vegetable 30
  Beetroot and potato 25
  Creole potato 17, 32
  Curried potato and apple 27
  Danish potato and herring 31
  Delano 34
  Dilled potato 25
  Hot potato 23
  Hot potato and parsley 24
  Mixed with peanut and chilli dressing 28
  Oriental potato 22
  Piquant potato with fennel 23
  Potato 22
  Potato and chilli 26
  Potato and herb 25
  Potato and orange 29
  Potato and tomato with anchovies 32
  Potato and vegetable with bumbu dressing 26
  Potato and white fish 34
  Potato and white radish 29

  Potato broad bean and yogurt 30
  Potato kiwi and fish 34
  Potato purée 22
  Potato ring 29
  Potato with peanut dressing 28
  Potato with rollmops 32
  Potato with wine dressing 21
  Winter potato 23
Spicy potato skins 18
Straw potatoes 19
Main meals and supper dishes 64–99
Aubergine and potato bake 86
Bubble and squeak 66
Cabbie claw 80
Cakes
  Chicken and sweetcorn potato 85
  Kipper 80
  Potato sandwich 70
Casseroles
  Beef with potatoes 90
  Lamb with potatoes and gin 91
  Lincolnshire pork 94
  New potato and chicken 89
  Potato and spinach 78
  Potato and turnip 79
Chilli and red cabbage with savoury potato topping 98
Clapshot 66
Cobbler, potato 72
Colcannon 66
Coquilles St Jacques 83
Cullen skink 82
Curries
  Cauliflower and potato (dry) 79
  Potato and prawn 84
  Vegetable with yogurt 79
Dublin coddle 90
Dumplings
  Derry 86
  Potato and ham 85
Fish and potato eggs 80
Flan, spinach with potato pastry 76
Galician pote 89
Goulash, potato 87
Hot pot, potato and bacon 88
Iranian lamb and potatoes 91
Kailkenny 66
Kephtides, potato 71
Kookoo with potatoes and herbs 69
Leeky potato frizzle 88
Lincolnshire stovies 77
Mixed meats with olives, raisins and potatoes 94
Omelette, potato and breadcrumb 69
Paprika potatoes 69
Peppers, stuffed 92
Pies
  Old Kentish shepherd's 96
  Shropshire fidget 97
  Beef, beer and potato 97
  Chicken and egg with meatballs 96
  Curried eggs and potatoes 74
  Czech potato 74
  Old English fish 82

Potato and beetroot 72
Potato and cockle 82
Vegetable 72
Vegetable and cheese 72
Pizza, Mark's quick potato 76
Potato and pepper scramble 85
Potato and vegetables with chilli sauce 67
Potato cabbage and cheese bake 78
Potato chicken and sweetcorn aspic 98
Potato Lorraine 77
Potatoes with cauliflower and eggs 67
Potatoes with cheesy bacon 90
Potatoes, oven cooked with bacon 97
Puchero 89
Quiche, asparagus and potato 74
Rissoles
    Potato, meat and pine nut 84
    Spiced potato 71
Savoury potato nests 95
Scotch eggs, potato 71
Soufflé, cheese and potato 71
Stews
    Brunswick 88
    Fish 84
    Turkish lamb 86
Sweet and savoury carbanado 90
Swiss potato and cheese savoury 78
Turnovers, potato and cheese 77
Measurements 13
Measures
    American 13
    Australian 13
Oven temperatures 13
Pancakes, see 'Breads, scones and pancakes'
Pastries, see 'Puddings, pies, cakes and pastries'
Pastry, see 'Basic recipes'
Pies, see 'Puddings, pies, cakes and pastries'
Potatoes
    buying 10
    cooking, baked 11
    cooking, boiled without peeling 11
    cooking, fried 11
    cooking, peeled and boiled 11
    cooking, peeled and steamed 11
    cooking, roasted 11
    handling 10

history of 7, 8, 9
new 12
old 11
preparing in advance 10
sweet 12
types of 10
useful household hints 14
Puddings, pies, cakes and pastries 114–125
Cakes
    Orange sandwich 120
    Pineapple upside down 124
    Potato 118
    Potato and almond 118
    Potato apple 118
    Potato chocolate 117
    Potato madeira 118
    Spiced potato 116
Cobbler, rhubarb and potato 120
Fancies, potato 116
Pies
    Onslow 125
    Peach, potato and meringue 125
Profiteroles, chocolate 116
Puddings
    Potato and summer fruit 124
    Potato syrup and chocolate 124
    Steamed chocolate 122
    Steamed date 122
    Steamed fruit 122
    Steamed rich 122
Tart, almond 120
Salads, see 'Hors d'oeuvres'
Scones, see 'Breads, scones and pancakes'
Side dishes, see 'Classics'
Soups 36–47
Chilled potato and saffron with herbs 39
Cream of potato with brussels sprouts 44
Crécy 43
Crème du Barry 41
Curried vegetable 43
Fish 46
Fish and potato with tomato 47
Goulash with potatoes 46
Grated potato 38
Green 42

Ham, egg and potato 45
Jean Ross's potato and ham bone 45
Leek and potato 40
Light potato 39
Minted potato with croutons 41
Mulligatawny 45
Oyster 46
Potato 38
Potato and chervil 38
Potato and kale 42
Potato with butter and parsley 38
Spiced potato 39
Swiss style potato 41
Tattie hushie 41
Tomato, potato and onion 43
Watercress 44
Winter from Devon 42
With potato balls 45
Stock, Potato 140
Supper dishes, see 'Main meals'
Sweet potatoes 108–113
And walnut casserole 113
Cake 112
Candied 111
Candied Jamaican style 111
Charlotte 113
Creole pudding 112
Imperiale 110
Mashed 110
Pie 113
Pie, old fashioned 112
Pone 111
With almonds and sherry 112
With cinnamon and orange 110
Purée 110
Volume conversions 13
Weight conversions 13
Wine 136–139
Hock, potato 139
Potato and barley 139
Potato and ginger 138
Potato and hop 138
Potato and onion 137, 139
Potato and raisin 000
Potato, ginger and fruit 138

INDEX OF COUNTRIES

Argentina
Chilli and red cabbage with savoury potato topping 98
Puchero 89
Sweet and savoury carbanado 90

Australia
Beef casserole with potatoes 90
Piquant potato salad with fennel 23
Potato and onion medley 61
Potato balls 58
Potato cake sandwich 70
Potato soup 38
Savoury potato nests 95
Spicy potato skins 18

Austria
Goulash soup with potatoes 46
Hot potato and parsley salad 24
Light potato soup 39
Orange sandwich cake 120
Potato and cheese turnovers 77
Potato and ham dumplings 85
Potato apple cake 118
Potato fancies 116
Potato salad 22

Belgium
Beef, beer and potato pie 97
Chilled potato and saffron soup with herbs 37, 39
herbed potatoes 53
Minted potato soup with croutons 41
Potato salad with wine dressing 21
Vegetable and cheese pie 72
Winter potato salad 23

Bermuda
Sweet potatoes with almonds and sherry 112
Sweet potatoes with cinnamon and orange 110

Canada
Baked potato with pineapple yogurt and cheese filling 104
Chicken and sweetcorn potato cakes 85
Pineapple upside down cake 124
Potato and ginger wine 138
Potato, chicken and sweetcorn aspic 98
Potato, ginger and fruit wine 138
Savoury herb scones 132

Czechoslovakia
Czech potato pie 74

Denmark
Caramelized potatoes 55
Danish potato and herring salad 31
Potato and summer fruit pudding 124
Potato and white fish salad 34
Potato slices with caviar 20

England
Asparagus and potato quiche 74
Baked potato with horseradish sauce 102
Baked potatoes with beef and mushroom filling with horseradish 106
Baked potatoes with boozy prawn and pepper topping 104
Baked potatoes with lemon and chutney filling 103
Baked potatoes with savoury minced beef and tomato filling 107
Baked potatoes with turkey and broccoli topping 105

Bubble and squeak 66
Cheesy potato balls 58
Leeky potato frizzle 88
Lincolnshire pork casserole 94
Lincolnshire stovies 77
Mark's quick potato pizza 76
Old English fish pie 82
Old Kentish shepherd's pie 96
Onslow pie 125
Potato and chervil soup 38
Potato and cockle pie 82
Potato and hop wine 138
Potato chocolate cake 117
Potato crisps 19
Potato dressing for potato salad 21
Potato Lorraine 77
Potato salad ring 29
Potato stock 140
Puff pastry 140
Rhubarb and potato cobbler 120
Shropshire fidget pie 97
Steamed chocolate pudding 122
Steamed date pudding 122
Straw potatoes 19
Tattie hushie 41
Winter soup from Devon 42

Finland
Fish stew 84
Potato and turnip casserole 79
Potato soup with butter and parsley 38

France
Anna potatoes 52
Byron potatoes 59
Château potatoes 55
Chatouillard potatoes 52
Choux pastry 140
Coquille St Jacques 83
Crainquebille potatoes 62
Crécy soup 43
Crème du Barry 41
Croquette potatoes 57
Darfin potatoes 52
Dauphin potatoes 63
Duchess potatoes 57
Lyonnaise potatoes 61
Milanese croquettes 60
Oven cooked potatoes with bacon 97
Parmentier potatoes 51
Potato à la maître d'hôtel 55
Potato borders 57
Potato Chantilly 102
Potato purée 63
Potato purée salad 22
Potato quenelles with Parmesan 60
Potatoes à l'hongroise 60
Potatoes à la landaise 59
Potatoes à la paysanne 55
Potatoes lorette 56
Rissole potatoes 52
Sauté potatoes 50
Soufflé potatoes 50
Watercress soup 44

Germany
Brunswick stew 88
Potato and almond cake 118
Potato and raisin wine 139
Potato bread rolls 130
Potato cake 118
Potato goulash 87
Potato hock 139
Potato pancakes 135
Potato salad with rollmops 32

Greece
Potato, meat and pine nut rissoles 84
Stuffed peppers 92

Holland
Baked potatoes with smoked ham and
    pineapple topping 106
Casserole of lamb with potatoes and gin
    91
Cream of potato soup with brussels
    sprouts and bacon 44
Curried potato and apple salad 27
Grated potato cakes 135
Hot potato salad 23
Potato and bacon hotpot 88
Potato and pepper scramble 85
Potato, syrup and chocolate pudding
    124

Hong Kong
Oriental potato salad 22

Hungary
Paprika potatoes 69

India
Green soup 42
Mulligatawny soup 45
Potato and chilli salad 26
Potato and white radish salad 29
Potato bread 128
Potato chutney 21
Potato pooris 131
Potatoes with garlic and sesame 53
Potatoes with whole spices and sesame
    53
Stir-fried potatoes with broccoli 68
Vegetable curry with yogurt 79

Indonesia
Bean curd and cooked vegetable salad
    30
Curried vegetable soup 43
Potato and prawn curry 84
Potato and vegetable salad with bumbu
    dressing 26
Potato salad with peanut dressing 28

Iran
Iranian lamb and potatoes 91
Kookoo with potatoes and herbs 69
Potatoes with cauliflower and eggs 67

Ireland
Boxty bread 128
Champ 62
Colcannon 66
Derry dumplings 86
Dublin coddle 90
Oyster soup 47
Pratie cakes 133
Vegetable pie 72

Italy
Aubergine and potato bake 86
Delano salad 34
Spinach flan with potato pastry 76

Jamaica
Sweet potato Imperiale 110
Sweet potato cake 112
Sweet potato pone 111
Sweet potatoes candied Jamaican style
    111

Luxembourg
Baked potatoes with sour cream sauce
    102

Malaysia
Mixed salad with peanut and chilli
    dressing 28
Spiced potato soup 39

Mexico
Fish and potato soup with tomato 47
Leek and potato soup 40

Mixed meats with olives, raisins and
    potatoes 94
Potato and herb salad 25
Potato and spinach casserole 78
Sweet potato purée 110

Morocco
Potato, broad bean and yogurt salad 30

New Zealand
Curried eggs and potato pie 74
Candied sweet potatoes 111
Chocolate profiteroles 116
Potato, kiwi and fish salad 34
Potato madeira cake 118
Sweet potato charlotte 113

Norway
Dilled potato salad 25
Potato and onion wine 139
Potato croutons 51
Potato flatbread 128
White potato bread 130

Pakistan
Cauliflower and potato dry curry 79

Poland
Beetroot and potato salad 25

Portugal
Almond tart 120
Potato and kale soup 42
Potato and orange salad 29
Potato and tomato salad with anchovies
    32

Scotland
Baked potatoes with liver, mushroom
    and onion filling 106
Baked potatoes with sour cream and
    Parmesan filling 103
Cabbie claw 80
Chips 50
Clapshot 66
Crunchy roast potatoes 56
Cullen skink 82
Jean Ross's potato and hambone soup
    45
Kailkenny 66
Kipper cakes 80
Potato and barley wine 139
Potato, cabbage and cheese bake 78
Potato cobbler 72
Potato scones 133
Shortcrust pastry 140
Steamed fruit pudding 122
Steamed rich pudding 122

South Africa
Potato pancakes with bacon and banana
    135

Spain
Galician pote 89
Grated potato soup 38
Ham, egg and potato soup 45
Mussels with potatoes 33
Potato and breadcrumb omelette 69
Potato and egg mayonnaise 19
Potato fritters 19
Potato stuffed apples 27
Soup with potato balls 45
Tomato, potato and onion soup 43

Sumatra
Potato and vegetables with chilli sauce
    67

Sweden
Creamy fried potatoes 62
Fish and potato eggs 80
Hasselback potatoes 54